Anonymous

The Prophets of the Lord

Their message to their own age and to ours

Anonymous

The Prophets of the Lord
Their message to their own age and to ours

ISBN/EAN: 9783337036324

Printed in Europe, USA, Canada, Australia, Japan

Cover: Foto ©Lupo / pixelio.de

More available books at **www.hansebooks.com**

The Prophets of the Lord; their Message to their own Age and to ours.

SERMONS

PREACHED DURING

THE SEASON OF LENT, 1869,

IN

OXFORD.

BY

THE LORD BISHOP OF OXFORD. H. P. LIDDON, M.A.
W. J. IRONS, D.D. T. T. CARTER, M.A.
THE LORD BISHOP OF LINCOLN. THE LORD BISHOP OF DERRY.
J. R. WOODFORD, M.A. J. MOORHOUSE, M.A.
E. B. PUSEY, D.D. W. R. FREMANTLE, M.A.
VEN. ARCHDEACON BICKERSTETH.

WITH A PREFACE

BY

SAMUEL, LORD BISHOP OF OXFORD.

Oxford,
AND 377, STRAND, LONDON:
JAMES PARKER AND CO.
1870.

PREFACE.

THE subject of this year's Lenten Sermons is not only of the deepest interest in itself, but it has a most direct bearing upon the special needs and temptations of the present times. For it is one great temptation of the day to forget that with the Church of all ages she, too, is the inheritor of that "spirit of prophecy which is the testimony of Jesus." Nothing can more give her boldness in dealing with all truth, breadth of view to contemplate without shrinking all God's counsel and God's ways, and unflinching courage to stand for Him before a hostile world, than a thorough realization of the great truth that she does possess this prophetic gift. The Sermons in this volume can, I think, scarcely be read with care without their awakening this conviction: may it please God to arouse, strengthen, and quicken it.

I cannot this year finish these prefatory remarks without remembering that I shall not again preside over the preaching of these Lenten Sermons, or select their subjects or their preachers, and I cannot remember this without desiring to thank thus publicly those who year by year have helped me with these Sermons. The days we have spent together each year at Cuddesdon, in prayer and consultation for their preparation, have been amongst the happiest of my life. To the preachers who have freely helped me, men of the highest station and of the greatest gifts in the Church, I return my cordial thanks for their ready aid. I believe that in many ways and to many souls these Sermons have been eminently blessed, and I pray God to return to all who have taken part in the work blessings of His Fatherly mercy for what they have thus rendered to Him.

S. OXON.

CUDDESDON PALACE,
Nov. 15, 1869.

CONTENTS.

SERMON I.
(p. 1.)
The Prophet that " came out of Judah."
1 KINGS xiii. 26.
BY THE LORD BISHOP OF OXFORD.

SERMON II.
(p. 13.)
Daniel.
DANIEL xii. 10.
BY W. J. IRONS, D.D.

SERMON III.
(p. 29.)
Jeremiah.
JEREMIAH i. 18.
BY THE LORD BISHOP OF LINCOLN.

SERMON IV.
(p. 47.)
Ezekiel.
EZEKIEL i. 1—3.
BY THE LORD BISHOP OF LINCOLN.

SERMON V.

(p. 63.)

The Prophet at Bochim.

JUDGES ii. 4.

BY J. R. WOODFORD, M.A.

SERMON VI.

(p. 75.)

Isaiah.

ISAIAH vi. 8—10.

BY E. B. PUSEY, D.D.

SERMON VII.

(p. 95.)

Jonah.

JONAH i. 10.

BY H. P. LIDDON, M.A.

SERMON VIII.

(p. 125.)

Elijah.

1 KINGS xviii. 21.

BY T. T. CARTER, M.A.

SERMON IX.

(p. 137.)

Elisha.

1 KINGS xix. 12—16.

BY THE LORD BISHOP OF DERRY.

SERMON X.

(p. 151.)

Job.

JOB xiii. 15.

BY J. MOORHOUSE, M.A.

SERMON XI.

(p. 169.)

Haggai, Zechariah, Malachi.

EZRA vi. 14.

BY W. R. FREMANTLE, M.A.

SERMON XII.

(p. 183.)

Enoch.

HEBREWS xi. 5.

BY THE VEN. ARCHDEACON BICKERSTETH.

SERMON I.
The Prophet that "came out of Judah."

───◆───

1 KINGS xiii. 26.

"It is the man of God, who was disobedient unto the word of the Lord."

THE subject of this course of sermons has been chosen with special reference to some of the chief needs and difficulties of the present time. It will bring you into close contact with a great and most important part of the Word of God: for of it the utterances of the Prophets form a large element. And whilst it does this, it will, I believe, be found to bring out in the most striking manner many of the practical lessons which we at this time most eminently need to strengthen us against our peculiar temptations, and to instruct us in the ways of holiness. Further, it will lead us to examine, and I hope to remove, some special difficulties of the present day. For there is no part of God's Word in which these difficulties are oftener found than in the lives, miracles, and words of the prophets; and as many of these difficulties are based on misapprehensions of the real place and purpose of the prophetic element in the book of God, they are to a great degree capable of removal.

Men often, for instance, speak as if the mere prediction of future events with a view chiefly to the fulfilment of these predictions furnishing an evidence for the truth of the revelation which the Bible contains, was the chief function of the prophetic office. Now this is itself a great mistake. Fulfilled prophecy is of course an evidence for the truth of the revelation in which it is contained, for none but God can really foreknow the future. But this is by no means the direct end of the prophet's office. Rather is it an accident, though a necessary accident, of its exercise; and it cannot be treated as the main purpose for which the prophets were raised up, without degrading their office into that of formal and somewhat capriciously appointed witnesses to one particular truth. Their true place in the divine economy is a far grander one than this. From first to last they were raised up, primarily for their own generation, as peculiar witnesses for God; witnesses of His being; witnesses of Him as a personal God, ruling ever amongst men; witnesses for Him against all the false notions of deity which issued from the darkened heart of fallen humanity, and impersonated themselves in the gods many and lords many of heathendom; witnesses amongst His own people against the formalism which is ever ready to congeal appointed means of grace into charms, and to degrade words and commandments which are pregnant with life into a dull literalism. The prophets in their own day and generation did all this. They witnessed that this living, personal all-directing God was the Father of all spirits. That He was Truth and no lie. That His will was no capricious autocratic rule, but that law in fulfilling which the creatures He had made could only find their own true blessedness. They came forward to declare against the present temptations and promises of the world, that only in doing that will of His faithfully and thoroughly could any true peace be found. They were ever shewing forth to men the past, the present, and the future as one connected whole in which the personal God was with His servants. Their predictions of the future were not like the utterances of the old oracles, the declaration of some simple disjointed event which should come to pass, but the revelation of the typical character of the past and the present, and so of what that present would become in the future. Prophecy from their mouths was history carried on into futurity. Thus they were evermore raising men from the letter to the spirit, from the seen to the unseen, from the accidental to the necessary. This strictly practical mission formed the very basis of their whole office. They came as living men instinct with the Spirit of God, to the men to whom they spake, and addressed themselves to them, to their temptations, their needs, their darknesses, their sins, their possible deliverances. And it is just because they did in very deed speak thus to those to whom they were first sent, that they speak now to us. For evermore heart answereth to heart, as the features to the glass in which their outlines lie mirrored forth.

In this their true character as God's witnesses throughout the passing and ever-varying ages, we may find the key to all those recurring variations which we may trace in the particulars of prophetical development. Thus in exact keeping with his character as God's witness, the prophet sent to those outside the covenant bears some single warning, to the enforcement of which his predictive power is strictly limited. So Jonah preached to Nineveh when he called the sinful city to repentance, and declared that yet forty days and Nineveh should be overthrown. For this was practically all the prediction which the enforcement of his summons needed. So when prophets were sent to the ten separated tribes, it was with some special message; and it was by the requirements necessary for their fulfilling this special mission that the predictive power committed to them was meted out. We may trace this in all the prophetic course of those mighty witnesses for God, Elijah and Elisha. Great as were the miracles they wrought, and which it was requisite that they should work, as visible credentials of their message, there is no record of their predictive power reaching beyond the comparatively narrow circle of the lives or fortunes of the kings or people whom they were bidden to rebuke or to withstand. Contrast with these the prophecies of those on whom the gift fell in the comparatively faithful kingdom of Judah. What an horizon opens, for instance, before Isaiah. How is every fact around him a type of the future; how do the sufferings, the fears, the hopes, the deliverances of the righteous king and the faithful people lead on his eye to the great kingdom of God's grace, to the true Son of David on His throne, and to the deliverance of the whole race in the day of the consummation of all things. And how accordant with all this is the fact that in the Christian Church, where the Spirit is given in much larger measure, the direct predictive power of the undying line of prophets is altogether absent. For the prophet, if he was to be the bearer of a special message to the men of his own day, must of necessity be himself a part of what was as yet an imperfect revelation. And so prophet after prophet would reveal something more; some new type would be expounded; the horizon of prophecy would widen; its voice would more and more prepare the way of the Great Prophet yet to come, whose revelation by Himself, and by His inspired Apostles, would give the last direct utterances of the prophetic spirit concerning the future which thenceforth the prophetic Spirit in the Church would verify and explain, but never add to. For when the whole message was delivered, and the whole spiritual system completed, there was no room for that gradual development which had been hitherto the special work of prophecy. Still out of the old centuries would then come forth, as now they do to us, the voices of the old prophets, who in witnessing to those around them, witnessed also unto us, and left, like charmed voices hanging in the middle air, messages for all time, which the ever-present Spirit of the Highest should wake up into fresh sounds of warning, of promise, and of teaching, as the weary ages needed their ever-living application.

Now all this seems in a very special manner to be set before us in the history of "the man of God who came up out of Judah by the word of the Lord unto Bethel[a]." How that "word" was spoken unto him we are not told; the special charges from "the mouth of the Lord," to eat no bread nor drink water in the evil city, and to return by another way, all imply that it was in some way more immediate and direct than by the awakening the righteous anger of his soul against Jeroboam's calf worship. However conveyed to him, he receives the charge, and he obeys it. He sets out to bear his witness. We can picture to ourselves that journey from Judah,—probably from Jerusalem to Bethel. It involved the extremest peril. Of all men living, Jeroboam was one of the last to whom such a message could be delivered with impunity. He was so remarkable even in his youth for vigour, strength, and determination, that he had attracted the special notice of Solomon the king, and had by him been set

[a] 1 Kings xiii. 1.

in the difficult post of the exactor of taxes from the tribe of Ephraim. Since that time all the events of his life had tended to deepen the lines of his character. His sympathy with those whom the hard rule of Solomon oppressed had roused within him the ardent spirit of a reformer. Then, as there swept over that purer flame the risings of ambition, there blazed forth from his soul longings even for the throne of Israel. After this came the prophetic message reading out to him this secret of his heart's desire, and promising him its future fulfilment: " Thou shalt reign according to all that thy soul desireth, and shalt be king over Israel [b]." Then there fell on his young ambition the blight of Solomon's suspicion, and his own exile into Egypt. There for years he had to wait the slow wearing out of the wise king's life, with all the bitterness of delayed expectation eating ever more and more into his heart and souring his proud spirit. With the accession of Rehoboam he returned to the Mount of Ephraim, where he had lived of old in all but kingly magnificence. The folly of the young monarch, stirred up by his inexperienced advisers, raised at once a popular disorder, and Jeroboam became the head and leader of the discontented people. From that post it had been but a step to the throne of the new northern kingdom of the ten tribes of Israel. So far, with whatever debasing motives of personal ambition in the actors, the revolution had been "of the Lord." He was punishing at once the house of David and the tribes of Israel for their sins. Jeroboam had got the throne, and he would keep it, and not trusting with all his heart in the God of Israel, he sought, like other worldly men in whom some sense of religion still survives, to strengthen God's

[b] 1 Kings xi. 37.

arm by the arm of flesh. And so he fell into the great sin which at last, canker like, ate out his whole house. He feared that if the ten tribes according to the old law went up perpetually to worship at Jerusalem, their hearts would by degrees be weaned from the new throne and turn to the ancient dynasty of David. It was the natural fear of an usurper, and he set himself to guard against it with the most consummate skill of earthly policy. The new kingdom should have a new centre of national worship. He would build a temple which should rival that of Solomon, and establish a ritual which should surpass that of Aaron. He would consult for the ease of his people by sparing them these long journeys to Jerusalem, and he would gratify their taste for sensuous worship by letting them bow down before their fathers' God under the image of the sacred calf of Egypt. This, then, was the key of his whole system. Whatever threatened this, threatened the throne for which he had waited so long and suffered so much. And now he had come down himself to open with royal magnificence the new temple in this great border town of Bethel.

This was the man, at this crisis of his reign, in this very agony of his great device, whom the prophet of God was sent down to confront, reprove, and humble. Doubtless, as he trod that solitary upland road from Judah unto Bethel, he forecast within himself all the coming struggle. Doubtless he committed the keeping of his soul to the God whose message he was bearing. Doubtless as he drew near to Bethel, and thought of the abominations which were turning the house of the Lord into the house of shame, his heart burned within him with righteous indignation. Doubtless there passed before that opened eye visions of Jacob's communing at Bethel with his fathers' God, of the ladder reaching up to heaven, of the altar of remembrance, and of all that God had done there for the house of his fathers. All this doubtless was given to him to nerve him for his work of daring. See him thus prepared as he stands before the king. He is not a mythical utterer of oracles, he is a *man of God;* he is a witness, a witness for the God of Israel; a witness against sin; a man to whom the mouth of the Lord has spoken, that he may witness in his day, as you and I must witness in ours, against all unrighteousness and wrong. And he bears his witness. As before the great altar on the great feast-day of the king's own devising the king's own arm is raised to offer incense, from the dark unbidden form which, with the freedom that eastern licence for the whole prophetic family made possible, had thrust itself into the inmost circle of worshippers there woke up the awful voice of uttermost denunciation. It is the work of a moment, and quick as thought the arm of the wrathful king is stretched out to seize the prophet of evil, and the eager cry "lay hold on him" interrupts the settled course of the idol worship. Then Jehovah's power is seen. The arm reached forth against His messenger cannot be drawn back, and the doomed altar before the eyes of all is rent asunder. Only when the king's pride is humbled, and only in answer to the prophet's prayer, is the withered arm restored.

One phase of the prophet's trial had passed by, but another follows. He is bidden to the palace feast, and offered a guerdon of royal gifts. But his faith endures, he sternly rejects both, for it has been charged him "by the word of the Lord eat no bread nor drink water, nor turn again by the same way that thou camest. So he went another way." What a triumphant departure—how soon, alas, to be turned into shame. For he who had borne so much for the witness of Jehovah, whose ear had been deaf alike to the threatenings and the bribes of the open enemy of God, king though he was, listens self-deceived to the old prophet's voice, who wanted, doubtless, to refresh his own waning influence by the presence of the man of God; and who overtook him resting with lingering step beneath a wayside tree instead of flying from the city of destruction. He comes back, and eats the forbidden bread and drinks the forbidden water, and at once the soft suggestions of the tempter turn into the stern utterances of the accuser and the judge, for the dried-up bed of prophetic utterance in the old man flows again with now unwonted words of prophecy as he speaks God's sentence on His unfaithful messenger. To that sentence, it seems, he humbly bows; resumes, but with how altered a spirit, the sadly interrupted journey, and in the roar of the lion which beset his way, heard yet once again the voice of God's righteous jealousy for the honour of His great Name.

So the history ends, not with dooming the man of God to final rejection. The old prophet's craving to have his own bones laid beside his victim's seems to say how far more hope there was in such a death of chastisement than in his own hollow life of falsehood; and yet it does end with a deeply mournful "Alas, my brother!" with a fall from noble and high-souled obedience; with the tragedy of a sudden death of violence; with a carcase coming not into the sepulchre of his fathers; with his name dropped out of the record of the saints; to shew alike in his failure and in his success that the prophet was a special witness of Jehovah, and must from first to last discharge his high office, with all the glory or all the loss of such a high companionship.

Now from all this, surely, our great lessons are plain. First. There is from the beginning of the history to its end a witness of the presence with us all our life through of the God of truth and righteousness. Surely these words are breathing everywhere, " God is a righteous Judge, strong and patient; and God is provoked every day." We can see how—hidden at the time by the throng of men's plans, passions, strivings, and sins —the veiled form is ever amongst them, overruling all, judging all, succouring His own, most present with them in their greatest need ; we can see the security of every one who does indeed serve Him ; how danger and threatening only make that security the more evidently certain. We see the impotence of the greatest might when it raises itself up against Him. We see how schemes of the most subtle craftiness involve in themselves some unforeseen element of failure if they have not God's sanction; and we may read for ourselves that the life which looks the most prosperous and successful is, if He is slighted or opposed in it, in very deed an utter, certain, perpetual failure.

Again, beyond these general lessons there are one or two of most searching specialty of application. For next, II. How terribly distinct are the evil features of the old prophet who dwelt at Bethel. What a history is his of illuminations of grace darkened ; of visitings of the Spirit resisted and banished ; of the transition so easily accomplished from being a teacher to being a seducer, from being a prophet of the Lord to being a prophet of lies. Surely a terrible but a most needful lesson. For where are there not these " old prophets?" Men who came up it may be to this University with some high purposes and true aspirations ; who meant to witness for God but who have grown cold, idle, indolent, sensual, or unbelieving; who now meet younger men who come up here what they once were, and who meet them to destroy them; who can say, "I also am a prophet of the Lord, as thou art;" I had these high aims, but I found there was no maintaining them; who if not in open word, in not less open deed, prophesy against a life of prayer, and watching, and rule, and self-denial; who have a sneer for Lenten observances, and frequent services, and often communions, or for a life of purity, or for a simple childlike faith in God's Word and in His Church; who would bring back escaped souls to eat bread and to drink water in the resting-places of iniquity.

The teaching of such tempters is in very deed a doctrine of devils: and yet they abound, and do on all sides their work of death. Everywhere respectable godless elders, with a lowered standard and lying sneers, are amongst men and women of all ages, in all professions, and in none worse than in the holy ministry, the murderers of souls. Such a man chills the prayers, disarms the watchfulness, overcomes the scruples of others, and so leads them to the brink of the pit; and then, when it may be they have fallen into some more overt iniquity than that to which the teacher, with his cold temperament and respectable habit of sinning, is himself tempted, he is the first piously to fold his hands and say his "alas, my brother!" over the souls that he has slain. Terrible beyond all imagining in the great day of the account will surely be the opening of the old prophet's tomb; terrible the rising up beside him of the souls which he has slain.

III. And but once again. Is there not written as in a legend of fire on this nameless tomb the glory or the shame which must be the portion of every prophet of the Lord? How great are his ventures, how grand his triumphs, how irresistible his strength, how strict his account. This it is, this it must be, to serve the Lord of hosts, the jealous God. And this, my brother, is, as a baptized man, thy service; this must be thy risk. This may be thy glory or thy fall. Oh let us be in earnest in discharging it! Let us watch and be sober. Let us watch especially after successes. Let us beware of resting under wayside trees. Let us press on. Let this Lent see us crying mightily for God's grace; aiming blows at our besetting sins; resolutely determining to conquer some old evil, to win some new grace, to be more than we have been, prophets, witnessing amongst our brethren for the great God of righteousness, and truth, and love.

SERMON II.

Daniel.

DANIEL xii. 10.

"Many will be purified, and made white, and tried; but the wicked will do wickedly: and none of the wicked will understand; but the wise will understand."

WE possess in the Old Testament what have been described as the "remains of the ancient literature of the people of God." Their destiny—involving indeed the blessing of the world—seems primarily brought before us in this sacred volume: it describes to us, throughout, their origin, their development, their falls, and their future. To a great extent no doubt they are isolated, the people "dwell alone," and the special Revelation of the heavenly will seems to be theirs.

But after many ages we reach an epoch in their history, and they are providentially placed in contact with the outer world of the Gentiles; and in one part of their Scriptures which refers to that time, we learn that the message of divine Revelation was, in some wise, brought to the heathen. The great problem of human probation was doubtless being worked out under other conditions in previous ages, yet it is very slightly glanced at in the Hebrew Scriptures until the chosen people had been carried captive into Babylon; but in the book of Daniel, which dates from that captivity, it is broadly stated, and may even be said to be, at first, its subject-matter.

The former half of this book, extending to the end of the sixth chapter, covers the "seventy years" from the siege of Jerusalem by Nebuchadnezzar to Cyrus, and these chapters bring into prominence the Babylonian kings, and court, and people much more than their captives. It would almost seem as though the object of the presence of the Jews in Babylon had been to force their divine revelation on the attention of their conquerors. Glance a moment at these first six chapters of the prophet, reserving the remaining half of the book at present.

The first chapter represents four Jewish youths, Daniel and his friends, as trained for three years in the Chaldee language and literature, and introduced to the royal presence. The second chapter, with no further preface, records a dream of the heathen monarch, which had the result of discrediting the Chaldean religion, and shewing that the God of Israel was "God of gods and King of kings." An interval then occurs, of many years. Nebuchadnezzar had revisited Palestine, and destroyed the Temple of God; and returning home flushed with victory, forgetting his old dream, and probably despising his twice-subdued captives, he inaugurated a stately idolatry on the old site of Babel, the plains of Dura. The third chapter tells us simply how this attempt issued in the discomfiture of idolatry, and the proclamation throughout the empire, that honour should be given to the God of heaven as the Ruler of nations. The chapter closes, time passes, the captivity wears on, probation is pursuing its silent course, the same king is on the throne, and there comes another Divine interference; and this is the subject of the fourth chapter. The king is cast down, and is obliged at the end of his seven years' humiliation to record the whole event, and say at the close, "now I Nebuchadnezzar praise and extol the God of heaven, all Whose works are truth; and those that walk in pride He is able to abase." We hear no more of that great monarch. At the end of another generation his grandson Belshazzar, who had been reigning many years, is cast down, for his defiance of God. The fifth chapter is wholly occupied with this; and the sixth completes the vindication of the Divine truth in the person of the delivered Daniel, spared to watch all the events of the seventy years, from first to last.

I. At this point, the middle of our prophet's roll, let us pause, for we have here by itself a kind of whole. We see the ancient Church, long separated from the rest of the world, brought into contact with it by Providence, to live and work with it a while: and we are here told nothing of the events during all that sojourn in Babylon, except the sacred message brought, in such reiterated and significant ways, to that mighty empire of heathenism.

Those messages tell us that a great trial of men had ever been, and was yet going on, though beyond the pale of Revelation: doubtless "many had, from time to time, been purified and tried, and the wicked had done wickedly: and the wicked did not understand; but the wise did understand." We may well mark the varied phases of human trial in that old-world probation, in its governments, its religions, its disasters, and its revolutions, as one by one they are laid out by the Prophet, and here given for our instruction, in all these things, as well as for the teaching of those to whom first the lesson came.

1. For Government was a need of the world: it was a part of the plan of man's probation on earth.—Powerful rulers of the growing human family had risen, from

the earliest days, proclaiming by their very existence this great human need of organization and rule. The development ought to have been good and wise, but became corrupt and oppressive; and the strong acquired rule for the mere love of rule, and then followed the brute desire of conquest for conquest's sake, until everywhere the social and moral ideal of patriarchal days was unknown. Then the Nebuchadnezzars "dreamed," while the "darkness was over the face of the world." Uncouth visions of false grandeur haunted the slumber of the ages. Those "who would be great, and were even called benefactors," aimed simply at "power," and the animal instinct of domineering strength superseded that higher moral aim,—Government for the good of all.

For mere love of power, as such, has injustice and baseness in it; it belongs rather to our inferior nature*, and is repugnant to those rights of personal responsibility which should be reverenced in every man. To bring back to men the moral origin of social rule, the moral meaning of government was a first necessity for that oppressive heathendom. Thrones, sceptres, crowns, were something more than aggrandisements of tyranny; and the mighty monarch of Babylon, and all around him, needed to have that truth brought nigh to them; needed to have their waking hallucinations dissipated. They were disturbed by their own dream, and seemed to have lost the whole meaning of existence. The dream was incoherent in its structure, a "head of gold," and other parts of "brass and silver, iron and clay." This

---

* The coarse popular maxim that "knowledge is power" is a sign of the debased moral condition of many who aim to "know" not for the joy of wisdom, but for the use to be had of certain knowledge in the struggles of the lower life.

could not last. A better Dominion for man was surely in the Future. Now the sacred secret of this true rule for men was that which alone would solve the dream which the wisest of Chaldea could not even express. And this was the Revelation now first brought to this world's conqueror, that all true "power is of God." Nebuchadnezzar had come in contact with the people of God to learn from their prophet that which none of his wisest and best could teach him,—the meaning of himself and his high dreams: "Thou, O king, art a king of kings, for the *God of heaven hath given thee* a kingdom, and power, and strength, and glory;" and the great Babylonian felt perhaps for the first moment of his career the moral meaning of his own position as he acknowledged to the Hebrew captive: "Of a truth it is that your God is a God of gods and a Lord of kings, and a revealer of secrets, seeing that thou couldst reveal this secret."

2. But it is not only to interpret the world's imperfect dreams that the Church is sent into its midst. There is that which is every-day reality, and no dream at all. The world has always some object of homage of its own, some lofty and overbearing Idolatry to which it would compel worship. Its organized habit of life may be changeable indeed from time to time; it is not therefore any true result of conscientiousness, it even takes the place of conscience, and for the time asserts despotic sway over the individual. Sometimes it is yet more systematic, and meddles directly in the province of religious conviction. Perhaps the necessity of controlling the untaught religious instincts of the multitude led to the attempt in various ways to direct so powerful an agency as religion. But sooner or later a true conscience everywhere would have to refuse homage to the

"image of gold in the plain of Dura," and dare the furnace. Now, to confront the world's idolatries aright, and with success, this also was the captive Church's sacred work.

But it was necessary that the worldly power, thus overstepping its own limits, should be made to see and feel that the opposition to its idolatry had something more in it than bravery, something more than even a conscientious heroism. And there was a grace in that ancient Church of God that could achieve this. It not only could resist—for any stubborn zeal is equal to resistance—but it could touch the conscience of Nebuchadnezzar. Those three men were not alone in the furnace of the persecutor, and he saw the fact; tradition, memory, fear, ill-treated conscience, all may have quickened his gaze; and "Lo, I see *four men* in the midst," cried the amazed monarch, "and the form of the fourth is like unto the Son of God." Yes, it is God's grace to His true people that the light with them which is divine, flashes, at such moments, even on the conscience of the world, and wins the victory for His truth.

3. But warnings against the heathen oppressions and idolatries were not the only lessons which Israel taught in Babylon. There was something more to be done than interpreting the dreams, more than transitorily touching the conscience of the world. Even the prosperities of empire, the action of government when doing in a large measure its real work, must be regarded as moral. There was something to be taught, then, far beyond the elevation of first principles as to the use of power, and even beyond the correction of conscience.—There might be "a tree whose top reached to heaven," and whose "leaves and fruit were fair, and the shadow

thereof was a refreshment for all," and yet when it was surveyed by the "holy one and the watcher that came down from heaven," it was seen to be a luxurious growth, a social system unfavourable to the progress and health of man, and at Heaven's bidding it might need to be shorn of its secure luxuriance,—not indeed destroyed as yet, but "cut down,"—so "that it might sprout again." From time to time, the truth must be brought close to men by startling social events, that there is a Special Providence in our highest affairs— a power constantly over our own—a happy guidance now, or now a severe Nemesis. There is a perpetual Government of Heaven, and rulers, if wise, will learn that they have a part under that Providence which orders the world. If in the hour of present prosperity this is forgotten, some disaster will soon mark the moral crisis, and remind the world of the Higher Power than its own. And thus was the king of Babylon in the greatness of his glory struck down to the dust. Seven years of confusion for his people, and humiliation for himself, taught both him and them that there is a "Divinity that shapes men's ways." He was overawed, he was made "wise," by the present Deity. "The wise shall understand."

4. But finally; it is evident that there is a limit beyond which special providences may not adjust a decaying civilization. Probation must not be superseded. And there may come a time when what men call a Revolution, a total change of the social condition, becomes a necessity for human well-being. When luxury has reached its fulness and the passions and selfishness of the powers that are dominant are in full revelry, "their time is come." It may be a reign of softness and indulgence, so much acknowledged that history seems to pause on its few materials. No furnace is lighted now for con-

science; no questions of conquest are stirred; Belshazzar's day is the close of a smoother prosperity. Daniel had been practically forgotten and his friends out of sight. The queen-mother remembered him, and in a moment of perplexity thought that the prophet of God might be of service. Religion, far from being persecuted, was rather utilized by the court, and Daniel was put forward "to interpret" a little, and promised a "gold chain," and to be "third ruler in the kingdom."—And what of those past interferences of Heaven? Are they so forgotten that they have afresh to be brought to mind? And what of those past messages which the king's ancestor had felt? Are they subsided? And where those former dreams of greatness, and their interpretation? Linger they only as warnings which, unheeded, have but accumulated wrath? Then, nothing remains but to terminate a society and government so powerless for all the high ends of human good. Nothing remains but "Mene, mene, tekel, upharsin,"—'Thou art weighed in the balance and found wanting!'

When that came to pass in that old heathen empire, it was not only the ruler, but society itself, that had become corrupt; for no sooner had a Darius been placed on the throne whence Belshazzar had fallen, than the people and the courtiers would gladly have thrown God's prophet to the lions—only that God's work could not be so undone by man. That seventy years of Hebrew captivity had been the seventy years of the closing probation of Babylon; and the Median conqueror had to begin by writing afresh the old decree, that "in all provinces of his kingdom men tremble and fear before the God of Daniel, for He is the living God and stedfast for ever, and His Kingdom that which shall not be destroyed, and His Dominion shall be unto the end."

Wont as we are to read those graphic stories of the dreams of the Babylonian, and the fiery furnace, and the den of lions, we may too easily lose sight of the world-sent Revelation which they convey. We forget that it was worth a long captivity of God's Church, to bring to the world the lesson, that our probation here is all watched, all subject to the plan of "Him Who ruleth the armies of heaven, and among the inhabitants of earth," all leading onwards to the Kingdom "of righteousness, the Kingdom of the Son of Man." And though now, awhile, the wicked are free "to do wickedly, yet the wise may be purified, and the wise may understand."

II. It is time that we turn now to the last half of the prophet's book—from the Revelation for Babylon to Revelation for expectant Israel, as the close of her captivity drew nigh, and the eyes of the faithful among them were lifted to heaven for aid.

The remaining six chapters of Daniel are rather like episodes than connected series, though they belong to each other. Here we have visions, not of heathen kings, but of the favoured prophet himself, interpreted to him by an angel of God. There are, in the seventh and eighth chapters, visions of events which were already beginning to unfold themselves; and they are expressed in mystic imagery, (familiar among the prophets from Joel, Micah, and Isaiah onwards to the Apocalypse;) and the interpreting angel is here part of the vision in each case. In the ninth and three concluding chapters, we have what may be described as four prolonged extatic interviews. In these, the more immediate future of Daniel's own people, and the principal object in the remote future, viz. the Kingdom of

Messiah, are opened to the prophet. A symbolical language of heaven seems used by Gabriel and by a supernatural Personage, whose revelations were partly understood, and partly such as "the prophet could not understand." Nor need we wonder, if those also who now read what Daniel saw in vision, or in that angelical intercourse, "understand but in part," if it appears by the record itself that much of the meaning was intended to be "closed up, to the time of the end."

The visions of the seventh and eighth chapters occurred (we are first significantly reminded) early in the reign of Belshazzar; and this suggests that we should mark what was the position of events when there were yet some sixteen or eighteen years of captivity to run out. Belshazzar succeeded two predecessors whose brief careers had been cut short by Cyrus. That conqueror did not proceed at once to take possession of the empire of Babylon. There were other conquests to be first made, and difficulties to be overcome, before he would be ready for the final assault, for which both his own prowess and Belshazzar's effeminacy were preparing the way. Causes both moral and dynastic were at work, and the anxious Israelites and their prophets and elders must have been intent on the issue. Daniel saw at this crisis, in the "deep sleep" which fell on him, the approaching break-up of the empire of Babylon: but he saw more. He saw that there was no hope *after* that event, of such immediate triumph for his people as he had longed for. Beyond the coming kingdoms of Media and Persia and Grecia, which are described by name, a long vista of other monarchies, and events of a remoter future, are spread out and so described that Daniel could understand nothing but the great postponement of the final glory. It was all to be "shut up," for it was to be "for many days," and the prophet "fainted, and was sick." "His cogitations troubled him," and "his countenance changed [b]."

It appears, however, from the ninth and following chapters, that notwithstanding this heavenly teaching as to the delay of the kingdom of Messiah, the prophet hung over the possibility that prayer might find such favour with God, at the end of the seventy years, that events might yet "be shortened." He had pondered the prophecy of Jeremiah, and "he set his face to seek the Lord God" with renewed fasting and supplication, as set forth in the ninth chapter. This was probably just after his encouraging deliverance from the den of lions. As some answer to his prayer, he lived to see the decree of Cyrus issued, and slightly acted on; but his grander hopes were not gratified [c]. The same angel whom he had seen in vision, early in Belshazzar's reign, revisited him once more, giving the prophet in yet stronger terms God's message to him, that the "time was long,"—"seventy weeks" of years. Daniel fully understood this, he says, at last; but he "mourned three full weeks [d]."

The prophet revived from this inaction in consequence of some mysterious strength communicated to him; but the extatic state continued. It is described as a being touched by One "like unto the similitude of the sons of men," which enabled him to listen to the angel's talk. In great amazement he watches while the story of the "times of the end" is unrolled, until he is able to see no more, and he is told to "shut the book." He says, "I heard and understood not." The certain future of the Divine plan, and his own peace, are all that he is able to discern. And thus the prophetic visions end: "Go

[b] Dan. vii. 15, 28; viii. 17, 27.   [c] Ibid. xii. 6.   [d] Ibid. x. 1, 2.

thy way, Daniel, for thou shalt rest and stand in thy lot at the end of the days ᵉ."

1. Who sees not here, in this contrast between the first and the second parts of this prophet, that while present duty and past failure fill the revelation to Babylon, the Future, nothing but the Future, is set before the heart and mind of God's Israel? Alike before the old world and before God's people, there lay the one same great future—all events must lead up to that—"the Kingdom that cannot be moved," "the Throne of the Son of Man," the Eternity of the "Ancient of days:" but the world has to pause, and in some sense be passive, in its outer court; the people of God must reach onward, according to the law of a spiritual life.

The first half of our prophet's book deals with no details of the world's remote future, save only that it foretells that "Kingdom of God." Its message was to the present conscience, for present duty, in the scheme of moral Providence. But the second half of the book has, very gradually, to open to our faith an unknown Future. It begins with present events, and those already springing out of them. But as the prospect lengthens the imagery grows more dim, and the description more intricate. Still Daniel is able, notwithstanding his depression, to follow for a time the angel's teaching. At length, it becomes too hard for mortal mind, and he fails. As the scene fades off into the future, the language becomes more mystical, the scope for human responsibility more wide. Much might appear certain, when seen at the river Ulai, which had a halo of the Son of Man when transfigured at Hiddekel ᶠ. And then the Ministry of Angels in the future providential dealings with the world is sublimely spoken

---

ᵉ Dan. xi., xii.   ᶠ Ibid. viii. 16; x. 7, 10.

of, as never before. The mystery of Evil, as interfering for a time with the plans of good, strikes down the prophet's soul. He found there would be hindrances in the invisible world as well as in the visible—more things done than were "dreamt of in man's philosophy." Angels could only speak in their own angelic way of those frustratings for a while of the Church's future. Gabriel said, that certain pending issues had to be waited for, before he could do his part : and after this, all subsequent events swim before the eye of man as in a mist. One thing is clear in the farthest distance, alike to the vision of Nebuchadnezzar and the vision of Daniel : the final overthrow of this world's empires, and the final glory of the empire of God, "the Kingdom that cannot be moved."

2. And let us learn the great lesson for the Church, which is indeed our own, while moving onwards to that Day, when they "that are wise shall shine as the sun, and as stars for ever;" (to which our glorious Master adds, they shall "shine in the Kingdom of their Father.") Ten thousand thousand incidents of that Future must, to the last, wait on human wills. Nor let us be seduced by heathenish soothsaying, to think that things are so fixed beforehand as to anticipate man's Responsibility. It has been the snare of the Evil one in every age to persuade men to regard the future as mechanically ordered, and not morally. No falsehood of power more truly diabolical than that of fixed Predestination of moral issues has ever been imposed on bewildered conscience. For it was true to the heathen monarch, that he might have "lengthened his tranquillity by repentance[g]." It was true to the prophet of God, that the seventy years of His people's captivity might need to

[g] Dan. iv. 27.

be followed by seven times seventy years of further trial, before the glorious end should come as foretold [h]. It was true to the angel of heaven, that the "prince of the power of the air" might withstand him, and hinder his work, "for twenty-one days [i]."

Faith is guided by the visionary index of the angel's finger. It assures us, from a loftier view than ours, of the glorious end towards which all is morally working, beneath the eye of God. Things at no time proceed at random: at all times they work both according to the lower wills, and the higher plan. And "the crises and seasons are in the Father's power," though not expressible according to created forms of finite knowledge. 'Not even the Son,' (as St. Athanasius says [k],) 'in His creatureship, could know the unfixed future.' *He* only Who knows all the possibilities of being can have clear and sure design as to the future of moral agency. While in these visions of God panorama after panorama passes before the prophet's faith, it may be that extatic sense alone could discern all that he saw, and that the measurements of the future may have to do with other than earthly modes of thought; while yet enough is apprehended to mark the heavenly chronology, and teach both the prophet and us the lesson of a real Divine arrangement.

3. Even to the most passing gaze the representation of this volume of our prophet has a marvellous unity and order, in itself, and harmony with all the revelations of God. It does the inspired work for the world and for the Church alike; aweing the world to its present duty, and raising to the future ("in the Father's power") the faith of His elect. Those mighty monarchies, and their huge struggles of old; the working in them (as they knew)

[h] Dan. ix. 23, 24. [i] Ibid. x. 12, 13. [k] Contr. Ar., iii. 28.

of human wills, and also (as the prophet saw) of evil "spirits of the air;" the parallel fact, co-existing with the outer world's probation, of a chosen people working out a heavenly design,—then, *their* intermingling with the outer world's empires even to the end; and the coming of the Kingdom of Righteousness, and the Everlasting KING!—who feels not, while he sees this tumultuous ocean of moral being as if tossing and foaming around him, that there comes to him a sound across the flood, of "Everlasting Life" for some, and "Everlasting Shame and Contempt" for others! Who feels not, as he grows in emotion while he reads, that he himself has a personal interest in all this! Who feels not that he will have to stand in his own immortal lot, "at the end of the days!"

"Many will be purified and made white and tried; and the wicked will do wickedly: and none of the wicked will understand, but the wise will understand."

Abide calmly, O believer, with the prophet and the angel and the Son of Man, "to the end of these wonders." "Angels, principalities, powers, all are thine, if thou art Christ's,"—for "Christ is God's." It is thou who shalt "stand in thy lot," "purified," and by trial "made white!"

> " . . . And when the mighty ones go forth,
> And from the east, and from the north,
> Unwilling ghosts shall summon'd be—
> I in thy lot would stand with thee!"

SERMON III.

Jeremiah.

JEREMIAH i. 18.

"Behold I have made thee this day a defenced city, and an iron pillar, and brasen walls against the whole land, against the kings of Judah, against the princes thereof, against the priests thereof, and against the people of the land."

THERE are two prophets in the Hebrew Canon of Holy Scripture, whose history and writings may best be studied in connexion, as mutually illustrative of each other. Both of them were priests as well as prophets; both foretold the destruction of Jerusalem by the armies of Nebuchadnezzar king of Babylon; both were contemporary with that event; both survived it. The one dwelt among Hebrew exiles and captives at the river Chebar in Babylonia, and echoed the voice of the other, prophesying at Jerusalem. Both were signal types of the Lord of all the prophets, the Incarnate Word of God; both pre-announced the graces and glories of His Advent, and the building up of His Church Universal; both are exemplary and instructive to all, especially to pastors and priests of the Church of Christ, who are commissioned to maintain and to declare the truth in evil days, and to cheer fainting hearts with hopes of future victories, and who, though feeble in themselves, are assured of strength and support from above, if they are faithful witnesses to Him Who has called them to their work.

One of these two prophets is Jeremiah: the other Ezekiel.

It is my purpose now to speak of the former: the latter will claim our attention on another occasion.

The prophetic mission of Jeremiah at Jerusalem lasted about forty years, dating from the thirteenth year of the good King Josiah[a], and closing with the fall of Jerusalem in the eleventh year of his son Zedekiah.

These forty years of probation granted to Jerusalem, during Jeremiah's prophetic ministry, may be compared with the forty years, beginning with our Lord's mission inaugurated at the river Jordan, and continued in His Apostles sent by Him and filled by the Holy Ghost given by Him from heaven, and preaching of coming judgments to Jerusalem, until the time of its destruction by the armies of imperial Rome.

After the capture of Jerusalem by the Chaldeans, Jeremiah prophesied in a heathen land, Egypt; and, similarly, after the destruction of Jerusalem by the Romans, the prophetic work of Christ was extended to the heathen world.

There is no Hebrew prophet with whose personal character and history we are so intimately acquainted as Jeremiah. And yet the time, place, and manner of his death are not known. He vanishes from the sight in a mysterious manner. The Jewish rabbis supposed that he would re-appear as a herald of the Messiah[b], and in the ancient Christian Church it was a prevalent opinion, that Jeremiah would come again in the latter days to fight against Antichrist[c].

There is a moral significance in these popular tradi-

---

[a] B.C. 627. Jer. i. 2, xxv. 3.   [b] Cp. Matth. xvi. 14.
[c] Victorinus Pet., *in Apocalypsim*, xi. 3; Sixtus Senensis, *Bibl. Sanct.*, vi. ann. 346; Neumann, *Einleit.*, pp. 68—72.

tions. The spirit which animated Jeremiah still breathes and moves in all faithful witnesses, who prepare the way for the Second Coming of Christ; and among the prophets of the Old Dispensation none affords more instruction than Jeremiah, both by his history and writings, how they may best contend against the Antichristianism of the last times.

Let us contemplate him in this light.

1. First, then, we may observe that Jeremiah teaches us to plant our feet firmly on the solid and sure foundation of God's written Word.

You are aware that it has been alleged by some in our own days, especially by one [d], who has revived in England the sceptical speculations of some Biblical critics of Germany [e], that Jeremiah, being a priest, and having easy access to the Temple, and whose father's name was Hilkiah, (supposed by them to be the same Hilkiah the high-priest who is related in the Second Book of Kings to have found the Book of the Law in the Temple in the reign of Josiah [f],) was himself the writer of the book which was said to have been found there, and that the book in question was no other than the Book of Deuteronomy, which the Hebrew and Christian Churches have agreed for many centuries in attributing to Moses, and which was received as the genuine work of Moses by Christ and His holy Apostles.

Such theories as these, however groundless they may be, yet have their uses to the reverent and thoughtful student of Holy Writ. The allegations just specified may serve to remind us of an important truth. Not only is there in fact a striking resemblance between the prophecies of Jeremiah and the Book of Deuteronomy,

[d] Bishop Colenso.   [e] Von Bohlen, De Wette, and others. See the Author's Introduction to Deut., pp. 195—201.   [f] 2 Kings xxii. 8.

but the spirit of Moses lived and moved in Jeremiah [f]. Jeremiah's mission began as the mission of Moses began, and as the mission of all true prophets begins—in a confession of personal weakness, and in words of humility: "Ah! Lord God, behold I cannot speak, for I am a child [h]." Jeremiah's prophecies are impregnated with the Pentateuch. Many of the phrases and portions of them are not intelligible without reference to it, especially the Book of Deuteronomy [i]. The Book of Deuteronomy is like that written roll, of which his brother prophet Ezekiel speaks, which he was commanded to take into his hands and eat [k]. Deuteronomy was such a roll to Jeremiah. He took it and ate it. It passed

---

[f] Compare Genesis i. 2; Jer. iv. 23: Gen. i. 28; Jer. iii. 16: Gen. vi. 7; Jer. ix. 9: Gen. viii. 22; Jer. xxxi. 36: Gen. xi. 3; Jer. li. 25, &c.: Gen. xv. 5; Jer. xxxiii. 22, cap. xxxiv.: Gen. xviii. 14; Jer. xxxii. 17: Gen. xix. 15; Jer. li. 6, 50: Gen. xix. 25; Jer. xx. 16: Gen. xxv. 26; Jer. ix. 3: Gen. xxx. 18, 20; Jer. xxxi. 16, 17: Gen. xxxvii. 35, xlii. 36; Jer. xxxi. 15: Gen. xlix. 17; Jer. viii. 16.

Compare Exodus iv. 10, &c.; Jer. i. 6, 7, xv. 19: Exod. vii. 14; Jer. l. 33: Exod. xvi. 9; Jer. xxx. 21: Exod. xx. 8, xi.; Jer. xvii. 21: Exod. xxii. 20; Jer. v. 28: Exod. xxxii. 9; Jer. vii. 26: Exod. xxxii. 16; Jer. xvii. 1: Exod. xxxiv. 7; Jer. xxx. 11, xxxii. 18.

Compare Leviticus xiii. 45; Thr. iv. 15: Lev. xix. 12; Jer. v. 2: Lev. xix. 16; Jer. vi. 28, ix. 3: Lev. xix. 27; Jer. ix. 25: Lev. xix. 32; Lam. v. 12: Lev. xxvi. 6; Jer. xiv. 13: Lev. xxvi. 13; Jer. ii. 20: Lev. xxvi. 33; Jer. iv. 27.

Compare Numbers v. 11—31; Jer. ii.: Numb. vi. 5, &c.; Jer. vii. 29: Numb. xvi. 22; Jer. xxxii. 27: Numb. xxi. 6; Jer. viii. 17: Numb. xxi. 28, xxiv. 17, &c.; Jer. xlviii. 45, 46, xlix. 16: Numb. xxiv. 14, 16; Jer. xxvi. 8, 9: Numb. xxxvi. 7, 8; Jer. vi. 12, viii. 10.

"Vides, nullam Pentateuchi esse partem, quin in usum vocata sit. Simul consequitur, omnia, quæ de lege divina antiquitus data apud Prophetam dicantur, ad Pentateuchum referenda esse, ita ut Jeremiæ saltem ætate Judæis nihil de posteriori legis origine compertum esse potuerit."—Kueper, *Jeremias Librorum Sacrorum Interpres atque Vindex*, p. 48. Berlin, 1837.

[h] Jer. i. 6; compare the words of Moses, Exod. iv. 10, vi. 12, 30.

[i] See the excellent work of Aug. Kueper just quoted, and König, *das Deuteronomium u. d. Prophet Jeremia*, Berlin, 1839; Delitzsch on the Psalms, p. 606, and on Isaiah, p. 27.

[k] Ezek. iii. 1; for example, ii. 19, 34, vi. 2, &c.

into his very life-blood, and assimilated itself to his whole spiritual being. Jeremiah had a special mission to shew to the Hebrew nation that the Pentateuch had a living power for himself and for his own age. He throws himself back upon the Law, and grounds himself upon it; he appeals to its code as a divine standard of moral and spiritual truth; and he declares that the curses for disobedience which had been denounced in Deuteronomy nearly a thousand years before were now growing up and springing forth in vigorous energy, and were about to be fulfilled in all their terrible reality. But he also comforts them with the assurance that the promises made in Deuteronomy would be accomplished, if they turned to God with contrite hearts. Hence the prophecies of Jeremiah ring with a clear note of power which sounded forth in the book of the Law at Horeb and in the wilderness of Arabia.

2. A like use may be made of another sceptical allegation of modern times, with regard to Jeremiah's prophecies.

It has been observed with truth, that a great portion of these predictions, especially those concerning Babylon, Moab, and Edom, are reiterations or amplifications of the prophecies of his great predecessor Isaiah.

Hence it has been inferred by some, that either the prophecies of Isaiah were interpolated by the author of those predictions in Jeremiah, or that those prophecies in Jeremiah are due to an unknown author whom some critics dignify by the name of "the second Isaiah[1];" but who never had any existence [m].

[1] For an account of these theories of De Wette, Eichhorn, Ewald, Hitzig, Movers, and others, see Hävernick, *Einleit.*, pp. 223—236; Keil, *Einleit.* § 75; Kueper, 79—98, 106—155.

[m] See the Author's *Introd.* to Isaiah. pp. xvi.—xxi.

Such theories as these vanish before the light of truth.

Jeremiah, in the latter days of Jerusalem, stood forth in the midst of an unbelieving age, and asserted the divine authority of the written Word. He affirmed the Inspiration of Holy Scripture, and he did this by repeating the solemn accents of the Law and the Prophets, especially of Isaiah [n]. He did it by adopting those accents as utterances of the Holy Spirit, by Whom he himself spake; and by recalling the mind of a rebellious nation to their commands and threatenings, and in endeavouring to disabuse his contemporaries at Jerusalem of the fond presumption, that because they enjoyed great spiritual privileges, and were inhabitants of the holy city, and had access to the courts of the Temple [o], and offered sacrifices there, and observed the forms of its Ritual, they would be saved from the sword of Babylon; and in warning them that all the threatenings of the Law and the Prophets would now be executed upon their own heads [p] by the Chaldean armies, if they did not shew their reverence for God and His Holy Word, by confessing their sins, and by humbling themselves before Him, and by practical amendment of life.

Jeremiah, in the last days of Jerusalem, discharged a sacred office in repeating and authenticating the prophetic oracles of former generations. By his ministry the Holy Spirit gathered together His own words, uttered by former prophets, and gave them new life and light. Jeremiah's prophecies are like a beautiful tessellated pavement, in which the enamelled glasswork, and precious stones, and rich jewels of divine

---

[n] See Caspari, *Jeremia ein Zeuge f. d. Aechtheit v. Iesaia*, 1843, in der *Zeitschrift luther. Theol. u. Kirche*, 1843.

[o] See Jer. vii. 4.   [p] Cp. Keil, *Einleit.* § 73.

truth are inlaid and incrusted as in a sacred mosaic spread before the altar of some beautiful temple q.

In this work of authenticating Holy Scripture, and re-affirming the authority and inspiration of the Law and the Prophets, Jeremiah, who prophesied in the last days of Jerusalem, before its capture by the Chaldeans, was a forerunner of Christ, the great Prophet of the Hebrew nation and the world. Christ in His conflict with Satan at the Temptation overthrew him with three quotations from the Law of Moses—all of them from the book of Deuteronomy r; and in the days of His earthly ministry before the fall of Jerusalem, the Incarnate Word set His own divine seal on the whole written Word of the Law and the Prophets, that is, on the entire volume of the Old Testament, and assured the world of its divine Inspiration and Authority, and directed the attention of all to its sacred precepts and solemn warnings.

The prophet Jeremiah, by his example, has taught all in these latter days, whether we be preachers or hearers, that we must look back upon the past, that we must feed upon the oracles of God as our daily bread, that we must incorporate them in our whole moral and spiritual being, and that we must appeal to them as our rule of faith and practice, and must endeavour with God's help to build ourselves and others on that immoveable Rock, which no winds or waves will ever shake.

3. Another arbitrary assertion of the same recent criticism may also be specified here, in order that it may be converted to good by reminding us of another remarkable attribute of Jeremiah's character, which ren-

q See on Jer. xlviii. 1.   r Matt. iv. 1—10.

ders it specially instructive and exemplary to the champions of the truth in days of trial and distress.

It has been alleged, that some of the prophetic portions of Holy Scripture which foretell the sufferings of Christ, especially the fifty-third chapter of Isaiah[s], and the sixty-ninth Psalm[t], have no reference to Jesus of Nazareth, but were fulfilled in the person of Jeremiah.

True it is, that the language of that fifty-third chapter of Isaiah, and of that sixty-ninth Psalm, had a remarkable applicability to Jeremiah. But why was this? Because Jeremiah was not only a prophet, but a prophecy. Jeremiah is among the prophets what Job is among the patriarchs[u]. Jeremiah is the *suffering* prophet. He was a signal type of "the Man of sorrows." He was a figure of Him who suffered on the cross, and who conquered by suffering.

When therefore we read in Isaiah, "He is brought as a lamb to the slaughter[x];" and when we hear Jeremiah saying, "I was a lamb brought to the slaughter[y];" and when we hear the Psalmist say, "I sink in deep mire where is no standing[z]," and "let not the pit shut her mouth upon me;" and when we read of Jeremiah the prophet, that "they took him and cast him into the dungeon or rather the *pit* (it is the same word in the original as in the Psalm, and is repeated no less than six times in the seven verses of that narrative con-

---

[s] Bunsen, Ewald; see the Author's Commentary on Isaiah liii., Prelim. Note.   [t] Hitzig.

[u] As the writer has endeavoured to shew in his *Introduction* to the Book of Job, p. xii. Jeremiah is called by the Christian fathers the πολυπαθέστατος of the prophets, Isidor. Pelusiot., *Epist.*, 298; and this qualified him to be what he is also called by them, the συμπαθέστατος; see Greg. Nazian., *Orat.* x.; cp. Heb. ii. 18, concerning Jeremiah's divine Anti-type, Jesus Christ.

[x] Isa. liii. 7.   [y] Jer. xi. 19.   [z] Ps. lxix. 2, 15.

cerning Jeremiah[a]) "and they let down Jeremiah with cords, and in the pit there was no water, but mire; so Jeremiah sunk in the mire:" when we hear and read such words as these, and many others in Jeremiah's history[b], and when also we remember that Jeremiah was cast into the pit and left to die there (as far as they were concerned) by the rulers of Jerusalem, and was drawn up out of the pit by a Gentile stranger, the Ethiopian eunuch Ebed-melech (as the Gospel of Christ, rejected and put to death by the Jews, was gladly received by the Gentiles[c]), we are brought to the conclusion, which is confirmed by countless incidents in Jeremiah's life, that in his history we have a foreshadowing of the Gospel, and that in seeing the struggles of Jeremiah standing alone against princes, prophets, priests, and people, and contending as a faithful witness of the truth, amid scorn, calumny, and insult, injury and violence; and foretelling the fall of Jerusalem in his prophecies, and yet weeping amid its ruins in his Lamentations, we have a vision of the agony in

---

[a] Cp. Lam. iii. 3, 55, where the same word is used.

[b] As e.g. Jer. xx. 27, "I am in derision daily, every one mocketh me;" cp. Ps. xxii. 7: and again, "They devise devices against me, saying, Let us destroy the tree with the fruit thereof; let us cut him off from the land of the living, that his name may be no more remembered:" see on xi. 19: and xxvi. 11, "Then spake the priests, This man is worthy to die," (cp. Matt. xxvi. 61, 66): and xxvi. 15, "If ye put me to death ye shall surely bring innocent blood upon yourselves, and upon this city, and upon the inhabitants thereof:" (cp. Matt. xxvii. 25). The prophecy concerning Christ's betrayal for thirty pieces of silver appears to have been delivered originally by Jeremiah, see below on Matt. xxvii. 9; see also Del Rio *Proleg. in Threnos*, cap. ii. S. Jerome (on xi. 18, 19) following Justin Martyr, Tertullian, and Cyprian says, "Omnium Ecclesiarum est consensus ut sub persona Jeremiæ a Christi hæc dici intelligant:" an assertion to be explained from St. Peter's assertion that the Spirit of Christ spake in the prophets, especially concerning His sufferings, and the glory that would follow, (1 Pet. i. 11).

[c] See Jer. xxxviii. 12, 13.

Gethsemane, and of the arraignment in the hall of Caiaphas, and of the precious death on Calvary, of Him who shed tears of compassion over Jerusalem, and who shed His Blood upon the Cross, to redeem her from her sins[d].

The ancient Hebrew Church appointed the Lamentations of Jeremiah to be continually repeated year after year on that solemn fast-day in the fifth month when she mourned for the destruction of Jerusalem by the Chaldean armies, and for her own sins which caused that desolation; a day made more memorable by the second capture of Jerusalem by the legions of Rome under Titus on the same anniversary. And the Christian Church, from ancient days, has set apart the Lamentations of Jeremiah for her own solemn offices in the week of her Lord's Passion[e]; and in contemplating the prophet Jeremiah sitting amid the ruins of Zion and pouring out his sorrow there in piteous cries of agony, she has ever had a vision of Christ hanging upon the Cross, and mourning over the ruins of our fallen human nature, which caused the bitterest pangs of His anguish there.

4. This typical adumbration of Christ in Jeremiah's sufferings, is not only a beautiful spiritual picture of the deepest pathos, but it has a living reality and practical power. There is no prophet in the Old Testament whose life, as displayed in his writings, extends over so long a period in a time of great public difficulty, and with whom we are so familiar as Jeremiah. His prophecies are his autobiography. They reveal the inmost workings of his soul from his youth to his old

---

[d] On the typical character of Jeremiah cp. A Lapide, *Proleg. in Jeremiam*, p. 496: "quot et quibus in rebus Jeremias fuerit typus Christi."

[e] On Maundy Thursday, Good Friday, and Easter Even. See *Introd. to Lamentations*.

age. He does not conceal from us his weaknesses [f]. "I am a child," he says, "I cannot speak [g]." He does not disguise from us his impatience and his disappointments; he reveals his feelings of discontent, and records his words of murmuring: "Woe is me, my mother, that thou hast borne me a man of strife and contention to the whole earth [h]!" He does not hide from us, that, like the prophet Jonah, he shrank back from his prophetic work; through fear of scorn, and insult, and persecutions, not only from men in high place and power, but even from his own friends and relations in his native town, Anathoth. His brethren, he tells us, the house of his father, dealt treacherously with him, and sought his life, and said, "Prophesy not to us in the Name of the Lord, that thou die not by our hand [i]." And therefore he exclaimed: "Oh that I had in the wilderness a lodging-place of wayfaring men; that I might leave my people, and go from them [k]." He was also bitterly distressed by the seeming failure of his own prophecies and of his ministerial labours: "Behold they say unto me, Where is the Word of the Lord? let it come now [l]." He is staggered and perplexed by the fact, that he himself, the prophet of the Lord God of Israel, is the victim of injury, and that his enemies and the adversaries of the Lord triumph over him. "Wherefore," he asks, "doth the way of the wicked prosper wherefore are all they happy that deal very treacherously [m]?" He complains of his seeming desertion by God: "Why is my pain perpetual and my wound incurable, which refuseth to be healed? wilt Thou, O God, be to me altogether as a liar, and as waters that fail [n]?" He expostulates and remonstrates with God, saying that he had not coveted

[f] Jer. xii. 6. [g] Ibid. i. 6. [h] Ibid. xv. 10. [i] Ibid. xi. 20.
[k] Ibid. ix. 2. [l] Ibid. xvii. 15. [m] Ibid. xii. 1. [n] Ibid. xv. 18.

the prophetic office, and had not desired to be a messenger of woe to his people º, and that he had been constrained to utter his prophecies by the overpowering force of God. "I said, I will not make mention of Him, nor speak any more in His Name. But His word was in mine heart as a burning fire shut up in my bones, and I was weary with forbearing and could not stay. For I heard the defaming of many, fear on every side. All my familiars watched for my halting ᵖ." And in a moment of despondency and anguish of soul, like another Job, he cursed the day of his birth: "Cursed be the day wherein I was born; let not the day wherein my mother bare me be blessed. Cursed be the man who brought tidings to my father, saying, A man child is born unto thee; making him very glad ᵠ."

Nor was this all. Jeremiah was commanded to go forth and declare God's sternest judgments on Jerusalem; and yet he was a man of the most loving spirit, and tender affection. His heart was well-nigh bursting with sorrow when he thought of the terrible message which he was ordered to deliver. What a wonderful depth of sympathy is there in that piteous ejaculation, "Oh that my head were waters, and mine eyes a fountain of tears, that I might weep day and night for the slain of the daughter of my people ʳ!"

5. Brethren, these things are full of instruction to ourselves. Each of us, whatever our calling, has a commission from God. Each has a message from Him to deliver, in evil days. In a certain sense, we are all Jeremiahs. And this is specially true with regard to some among us. You, my younger hearers, who are candidates for the sacred ministry, will often feel as he felt. You may often find yourselves saying within

---

Jer. xvii. 16.   ᵖ Ibid. xx. 9, 10.   ᵠ Ibid. xx. 14.   ʳ Ibid. ix. 1.

yourselves, "I am a child and cannot speak." When you are called upon to encounter dangerous error and to reprove deadly sin; when it is your duty to stand forth as Jeremiah among the many, the powerful, and the great; whenever it is your mission to denounce God's judgments upon that dangerous error or deadly sin, although that error and sin may be patronized by some who are greatly your superiors in age and station, and, it may be, in intellectual gifts, and literary and scientific attainments, you may then perhaps feel your heart sink within you, and may ask yourself the question, Who am I that I should do this? You may long to retire from your post at Anathoth or Jerusalem, and may sigh for some lodge in the wilderness[s]. You may perhaps be tempted to repine at your lot, and even to murmur at God, for calling you to the priestly and prophetical office; and to arraign the dispensations of His providence in allowing wickedness to prosper, and in seeming to forsake His ministers, and to allow His truth to fail. Do not be surprised at this. Strange it would be, if in times of severe trial such emotions as these did not sometimes arise within you. They were felt by Jeremiah. But remember him: think of his sufferings. He stood alone in a godless age. God did not allow him to take to himself a partner of his sorrows. He had no wife to comfort him[t], as Isaiah had[u]. His own flesh and blood forsook him. His own fellow-townsmen of Anathoth sought his life and hooted at him in the streets[x], and went about to kill him as a false prophet. He was smitten and put in the stocks by Pashur, who had chief authority in the house of God. The sanguinary King Jehoiakim sought his life, and

[s] Jer. ix. 2.   [t] Ibid. xvi. 2.   [u] Isa. vii. 3, viii. 3.
[x] Jer. xi. 19—21, xii. 6.

the weak and vacillating Zedekiah surrendered him to his enemies. At first some of the princes interceded for him; but they also forsook him, and conspired with the priests and false prophets against him. At the close of his forty years' mission, when the Chaldeans were at the gates, and Jerusalem was near her fall, they cast the prophet into the pit, or cistern, of the state prison, and left him there to sink in the mire and starve. And the only person in the holy city, Jerusalem, who was found to have pity on God's prophet Jeremiah was a stranger, an Ethiopian eunuch, Ebedmelech.

Observe now this. Jeremiah's words of weakness, timidity, and impatience belong to the earlier stage of his career. As his sufferings became more intense he received more grace from God, and gained fresh courage, and derived inspiration from difficulty and danger. As time passed on, he who once himself had faltered was enabled to encourage others. His dear friend and secretary, Baruch, seems to have been a person of honourable family; Baruch's brother Seraiah attained to a high position as chamberlain[y] in the court of Zedekiah, and enjoyed the royal favour; and Baruch appears to have had some ambitious desires, and to have aspired to advancement in public life. But his connexion with Jeremiah, the stern reprover of courtly and princely vices, frustrated his hopes and obstructed his rise. Baruch was a faithful and steadfast friend to Jeremiah, and executed his commands in writing and reading the prophetic roll which denounced woe on the princes and people of Jerusalem[z]. Baruch's life was threatened as well as that of Jeremiah; and he murmured for the failure of all earthly hopes, and he shrank

[y] See below on Jer. li. 59—61.   [z] Jer. xxxvi. 4—32.

back with fear, and said, "Woe is me! the Lord hath added grief to my sorrow: I fainted in my sighing, and I found no rest [a]." Then Jeremiah assured him of protection, and consoled him for the loss of worldly advancement: "Seekest thou great things for thyself? seek them not [b]."

6. Yet further, Jeremiah the prophet of suffering, not only was enabled by God to triumph over difficulty and danger, and to give comfort to his own friends in distress, but he was also a divine minister of consolation and joy to the whole Hebrew nation, whether in the city of Jerusalem or scattered throughout the world. He cheered them with bright hopes of the future, and with glorious promises of Him, Whose Gospel was to go forth from Zion to gladden the hearts of all nations. And it is surely a marvellous thing, that the most glowing prophecies of Jeremiah, concerning the future triumphs of the Gospel of Christ, and the glory of God's Church, (which was to have its origin at Jerusalem,) and the infinite joy and eternal splendours of the coming kingdom of Christ [c]: all blaze forth from the darkest cloud of the woes of Jerusalem, and from the thickest darkness of Jeremiah's sufferings. The midnight of his human sorrow was the noonday of his prophetic glory. The twenty-eighth to the end of the thirty-third chapters of Jeremiah, which foretel the graces of the Incarnation of the Son of God, and our justification in Him who is "the LORD our RIGHTEOUSNESS [d];" and the extension of the Church of God from Jerusalem to enfold all nations; and the eternal monarchy and priesthood of Christ [e]; and His victory over sin and death; and our resurrection to glory

[a] Jer. xlv. 3. [b] Ibid. xlv. 5. [c] See on Jer. xxxi. 22.
[d] See on Jer. xxxiii. 16; cp. xxiii. 6. [e] Jer. xxxiii. 17—22.

through Him[f]; and the spiritual graces of His Church; and the pouring forth of the Holy Spirit; and the blessings of the new Covenant of grace, and love, and peace[g],—all belong to the last days of Jerusalem, when the magnificent fabric of its Temple was about to sink into the dust, and its walls and princely palaces were about to be thrown prostrate on the ground.

Whence was this light from darkness?

It was the work of God's grace, given to the prophet's prayer, and working together with his will.

The *name* of Jeremiah, like that of the other Hebrew prophets[h], is significant. Some have supposed that it implies that he was *exalted* by the *Lord*[i]. Others assert with more probability that it means *set* by the *Lord*, as a solid foundation; or *sent* forth by the *Lord*, as lightning from the cloud, or as an arrow from a bow[k].

Whichever etymology we adopt, the name Jeremiah intimates, that whatever he did and whatever he suffered, all was *from the Lord*. The Lord worked in him, and by him. The Lord had said to him, "Thou shalt go to all that I shall send thee, and whatsoever I command thee thou shalt speak. Be not afraid of their faces: I am with thee to deliver thee. I have set thee over the nations and over the kingdoms, to root out, to pull down and destroy, and to throw down, to build and to plant. Thou therefore gird up thy loins, and arise, and speak unto them all that I command thee: be not dismayed at their faces, lest I confound thee before them. For behold I have made thee a defenced city,

---

[f] See Jer. xxxi. 15—17.   [g] Ibid. xxxi. 30, 31.
[h] Enoch, Elijah, Elisha, Isaiah, Ezekiel, Joel, Micah, Nahum, Malachi.
[i] S. Jerome, Simonis, Hiller, Venema; see Neumann, *Jeremias von Anathoth*, p. 8.
[k] Gesenius, 369; cp. Carpzov., *Intr.*, p. 130.

and an iron pillar, and a brasen wall against the whole land, against the kings of Judah, against the princes thereof, against the priests thereof, and against the people of the land. And they shall fight against thee, but they shall not prevail against thee, for I am with thee, saith the Lord, to deliver thee [l]."

This was the mission of Jeremiah, and he had grace to accomplish it; he stood firm for forty years, alone in a rebellious and godless nation of adversaries and persecutors. He was set by God's hand as a solitary beacon on a lofty tower, in a dark night, in a stormy sea; lashed by waves and winds, but never shaken from his foundations. He was insulted, mocked, beaten and imprisoned. His warnings were despised and rejected, but they were the words of God; his prophecy concerning the false prophet Hananiah [m], his prophecies concerning the last four kings of Judah—Shallum, Jeconiah, Jehoiakim, and Zedekiah [n],—were all exactly fulfilled in his own age; his predictions that Egypt, to whom the kings of Judah resorted for aid against Babylon, would not be able to succour her [o]; and that Jerusalem would be destroyed by the Chaldeans, and that Egypt itself would be subdued by them [p], were accomplished in his own times. The armies of Babylon, who burned the Temple and the city of Jerusalem, wrote, as it were, in characters of fire the evidence of Jeremiah's mission from God. Jeremiah was strengthened by these proofs of his own divine legation; but he was not elated by the abundance of his revelations, and by these signal tokens of God's special favour to him. No; though as a prophet he had been strengthened by God,

---

[l] Jer. i. 7—19; cp. vi. 27, xv. 20, 21.   [m] Ibid. xxviii. 1—17.
[n] Ibid. xxii. 1—30.   [o] Ibid. xxv. 19, xxxvii. 5—10.   [p] Ibid. xliii. 2—19, xliv. 29, 30.

and raised to a lofty eminence above all his contemporaries in Jerusalem, yet he still felt as before. He was still the same tender-hearted and sympathising man, the same loyal subject, and the same devoted patriot. His own sufferings made him more compassionate for those of others. The destruction of Jerusalem was the proof of his mission from heaven, but after that terrible catastrophe, Jeremiah went down from the heights of Mizpah, to which he had been conducted by Gedaliah the son of Ahikam, and he there sat down on the ground as a mourner amid the ruins of Sion, and poured forth his Lamentations over her.

ID
SERMON IV.

Ezekiel.

EZEKIEL i. 1—3.

"Now it came to pass in the thirtieth year, in the fourth month, in the fifth day of the month, as I was among the captives by the river of Chebar, that the heavens were opened, and I saw visions of God. In the fifth day of the month, which was the fifth year of king Jehoiachin's captivity, the word of the Lord came expressly unto Ezekiel the priest, the son of Buzi, in the land of the Chaldeans by the river Chebar; and the hand of the Lord was there upon him."

THE names of the Hebrew prophets have a sacred significance. Of the four greater prophets, two prophesied at Jerusalem—Isaiah and Jeremiah; and two prophesied in Babylonia—Ezekiel and Daniel. The names of the two who prophesied at Jerusalem, Isaiah and Jeremiah, are compounded with the divine Name JAH or JEHOVAH, the appellation of God as the Lord of the covenanted people, Israel. The names of the other two prophets, Ezekiel and Daniel, who prophesied in the land of Babylon—the great Empire of the world as distinguished from Sion, the Church of God,—are compounded with the sacred Name EL, which designates God in His universal supremacy as Creator and Ruler of all things, and which bears the same relation to ELOHIM as JAH does to JEHOVAH.

This assignment of names to these four great Hebrew seers was providential. As we have already seen, Jeremiah reiterates and authenticates the words of Isaiah, and, as may readily be shewn, not only did the prophet Daniel at Babylon and at Susa study the book of Jeremiah and refer to it in his own prophecies[a], and act upon the revelations made therein, and thus set his own seal upon the writings of Jeremiah, but the prophecies of Ezekiel are like a responsive echo[b] to those of Jeremiah. Both Jeremiah and Ezekiel were priests as well as prophets. Jeremiah is the prophet of the tenderest affections, Ezekiel is the prophet of the most fervid imagination; Jeremiah is more than the Euripides, Ezekiel is more than the Æschylus, of Hebrew prophecy. Ezekiel, at the river Chebar in northern Mesopotamia, bore witness to the divine utterance which came from Jeremiah at Jerusalem. The prophet Jeremiah at Jerusalem was set there by God to be a faithful witness in an evil generation: "I have made thee to be a defenced city, an iron pillar, and brasen walls against the whole land, against the kings of Judah, the princes, and the priests, and the people of the land[c]." And to the prophet Ezekiel, among the Hebrew captives in Babylonia, God said, "Behold, I have made thy face strong against their face, and thy forehead strong against their foreheads; as an adamant harder than flint have I made thy forehead; fear them not, neither be dismayed[d]." The two prophets stood like two opposite cliffs hanging over intervening straits—such as Calpe and Abyla, or Sestos and Abydos,—confronting one another, rising above the swell of the ocean, and dashed upon by a stormy sea rolling between them.

[a] Dan. ix. 2. Compare Jer. xxv. 11, xxix. 10.

[b] Compare Jer. i. 13 with Ezek. xi. 3, 8, xxiv. 2; Jer. iii. 6—11 with Ezek. xvi. 46—51, xxiii. 11; and see the present writer's notes on Ezek. iv. 3, xi. 16, xiii. 2, 3, xiv. 14, xxxii. 19.

[c] Jer. i. 18. [d] Ezek. iii. 9.

This phenomenon displays a truth which ought ever to be present to the mind of the student of Hebrew prophecy. All the prophets, in whatever time and in whatever land they lived, prophesied by one and the same Spirit; and, as St. Peter affirms, that Spirit was the Spirit of Christ. St. Peter says that the prophets "searched diligently, what the *Spirit of Christ*, which was in them, did signify, when it testified beforehand the *sufferings* of Christ and the *glory* that should follow[e]."

This apostolic sentence is the clue to all right prophetic interpretation. The Spirit in all the prophets was the Spirit of Christ, and it testified of His sufferings and of the glory that would follow from them.

This truth is displayed in the names, persons, and prophecies of the four greater Hebrew prophets. Isaiah, which means the *salvation of Jehovah*, is the first Hebrew prophet who calls the Messiah *the servant of the Lord*, and he sets before us more clearly than any other of his predecessors the Passion of Christ. Jeremiah, as we have seen, is the prophet of suffering, and his prophecies are followed by a national dirge in his Lamentations. He is the type of the *Christus patiens*. But Ezekiel is the prophet of the glory that would follow the suffering. The prophecies of Ezekiel are introduced with a revelation of glory. He himself a priest, called to his prophetic office at the river Chebar in his *thirtieth* year[f], and designated by God throughout his prophecies as *Son of Man*, (which no Hebrew pro-

---

[e] 1 Pet. i. 11.
[f] Ezek. i. 1. Ezekiel began to prophesy on the fifth day of the fourth month of the fifth year of the captivity at Babylon of king Jehoiachin or Jeconiah (B.C. 595); the fifth year of his successor, Zedekiah; and about seven years before the destruction of Jerusalem by the Chaldeans in the thirteenth year of Nebuchadnezzar (B.C. 588). Ezekiel continued to prophesy for at least twenty-two years. See xxix. 17, xl. 1.

phet who prophesied at Jerusalem ever is ^k) ; and seeing the heavens opened, and beholding visions of God's glory, is a signal type of the Incarnate God, "the Son of Man," standing, in His thirtieth year, at the river Jordan, and inaugurated there as Prophet, Priest and King, when, as the Gospel says, "the heavens opened unto Him, and He saw the Spirit of God descending like a dove and lighting upon Him, and lo! a voice from heaven, saying, This is My beloved Son, in whom I am well pleased ^h."

Jeremiah's prophecies begin and end with a vision of suffering; Ezekiel's prophecies begin and end with a vision of glory. The last nine chapters of Ezekiel describe the visionary Temple and the ideal Holy Land, in a mysterious transfiguration, and are prophetic representations of the grace and glory of the Catholic Church, and are like a prelude to the visions of the Apocalypse, and the splendours of the new Jerusalem.

His brother prophet, Daniel, at Babylon completes this glorious picture, by his descriptions of the Second Coming of Christ, and the general Resurrection, and the Judgment of quick and dead ⁱ, and the bliss of the saints in glory. And thus the two great prophets of the exile and the captivity of Israel are also the two great prophets of everlasting peace and heavenly joy of the Church of Christ.

The sufferings of Christ as revealed by Isaiah and Jeremiah, the two greatest prophets who prophesied at Jerusalem, and whose names are compounded with the sacred appellation of JAH or Jehovah, the Lord God of Israel, the God of the Hebrew Church, lead on by

---

^g Daniel, who did not prophesy at Jerusalem, is once so called, viii. 17.
^h Matt. iii. 16, 17; Mark i. 10, 11; Luke iii. 21—23.
ⁱ Dan. vii. 9—14, xii. 2.

a beautiful transition to the glories of Christ, which followed those sufferings, and which are revealed in Ezekiel and Daniel, who prophesied in a heathen land, and whose names,—one, that of Ezekiel, referring to the *strength* of God, and the other, that of Daniel, to the *judgment* of God,—are compounded with EL, the Hebrew designation of God the Creator in His Universal Supremacy, and who unfolded in their prophecies the gracious assurance that although the material Jerusalem was levelled in the dust, and though the Church of God was in exile and captivity, hanging up its harp on the willows which overhung the waters of Babylon, yet the *glory of the Lord* can never fall away, nay, it gleams forth more brightly from the gloom of sorrow and suffering, it derives fresh life from death, and a new creation from destruction. Although banished from Jerusalem, it is diffused into the heathen world, which has become a temple and city of God, and is a place of preparatory probation for the Church glorified in heaven.

Ezekiel, whose prophetic designation is "Son of Man," is the priest and prophet, not of the temple and city of Jerusalem, but of the spiritual temple of universal humanity. This is his great value: he catholicizes Hebraism. He leads us on to contemplate and adore the Lord God of the Old Testament in all the breadth and depth and height of His divine attributes, as Universal Father and Saviour of all.

Observe how he displays God's Omnipresence and Omniscience.

A short time before the destruction of Jerusalem, Ezekiel, the captive prophet in exile on the banks of the river Chebar, being severed, at a distance of more than 400 miles on the north-east, from Jerusalem, was enabled, by the Holy Spirit, to behold and to describe the strange mysteries of impure worship which were celebrated in the secret chambers and dark crypts of the Temple there; his inner eye was illumined by the Spirit of God, and he was enabled to specify by name the men who were standing there with censers in their hand, and raising a thick cloud of incense, through the misty veil of which he descried the vermilion paintings on the wall, of grotesque figures of creeping things and abominable beasts of Egyptian idolatry in the chambers of their imagery; he was enabled to see the women mimicking the ritual of Phœnicia and weeping for the Syrian Thammuz, or Adonis, in the courts of the Lord God of Israel; and he saw the men between the porch and the altar in Sion turning their backs on the Temple of Jehovah, and bowing down their heads in lowly adoration to worship the rising sun [k].

The prophet Ezekiel, dwelling in exile in Babylon, was also enabled to foresee and describe the scene of that last fatal night of Jerusalem besieged by the Chaldean army, when the last king of Judah, Zedekiah, who had mocked the warnings of the prophet Jeremiah, stole secretly out of his palace with a few attendants, and passed along through the gate between the two walls which were by the king's garden, with his face muffled up in his mantle [l], and was caught, as it were, in a net, with his companions, by his Chaldean enemies in the plain of Jericho.

Not merely was Ezekiel enabled to see these things, and to describe them, but he was commanded to shew his faith in his own inspiration by *enacting* them in the presence of the captives in Babylon. He was commanded to pourtray the siege of Jerusalem by a picture drawn with chalk on a dark brick of Babylon [m], and to

[k] See Ezek. viii. 8—16. [l] See Ezek. xii. 12, 14.
[m] See Ezek. iv. 1, 3.

represent its blockade by visible actions; and he was commanded to shew his faith in his own revelations from God by removing his own furniture from his own house in Babylon [n] in the dim twilight, as a token that Zedekiah, the king of Judah, would in like manner go forth in the dusk of the evening from his palace; and he was ordered to declare the meaning of these prophetic actions to those who were with him in Chaldæa, so that, if these symbolical actions had not been realized by that which they were intended to symbolize, Ezekiel would have become a laughing-stock to the captives, and been rejected with scorn by the Hebrew nation, and have never been received by them as an inspired prophet of God.

Ezekiel *was* recognised as such by the Hebrew Church; he was owned as such by Christ and His Apostles. And therefore these words and acts of Ezekiel preach to us and to all the world the great doctrines of the Divine Omnipresence and Omniscience, and of our own personal responsibility.

If Ezekiel, at the river Chebar, was enabled by God to reveal the hidden things of the secret chambers of the Temple at Jerusalem, and to specify by name the persons who were there engaged in those unhallowed mysteries, and to see through the thick cloud of the incense which enveloped them; can it be supposed that there is anything in the inmost recesses of our own hearts which the eye of Ezekiel's God does not penetrate and pierce? Can it be imagined that there is any idolatry—carnal, intellectual, or spiritual—which we ourselves practise in the secret crypts and subterranean chambers of the imagery of our own thoughts, which is not clear as noon-day to His view?

[n] See Ezek. xii. 3—15.

And can it be imagined that there is anything which He will not bring forth to judgment as He brought forth the men of Jerusalem to be judged by the Man, an impersonation of Christ, whom Ezekiel saw clothed in linen, with a writer's ink-horn at his side, to note down, in a book, the actions of the princes and people at Jerusalem, and who executed sentence upon them, and who also set His mark—a mark, it was, of the cross [o]—on the forehead of every one, who sighed, cried, and mourned over their hateful abominations, in order that they might be spared in the terrible slaughter which destroyed the rest [p]?

This prophetic representation of the divine attributes of Omnipresence and Omniscience is combined in Ezekiel with a solemn declaration of the utter hollowness of all mere formal, ceremonial, worship; and of the necessity of a deep sense of our own individual responsibility; and of the duty of searching self-examination and practical repentance, and of spiritual, vital, personal religion.

In the latter days of Jerusalem, before its destruction by the arms of Babylon (as afterward in the time of our Lord and His Apostles, before its destruction by Rome), the inhabitants of the Holy City relied on their religious privileges, and were elated with spiritual pride and presumptuous self-confidence. They vaunted themselves to be the national depositories and guardians of the sacred oracles of God. They were possessors of the Law, the Prophets, and the Priesthood. They dwelt in the Holy City, and worshipped in the courts of the Temple. They thought themselves safe there; they imagined, that because they themselves had been spared, while king Jehoiachin and the queen mother,

[o] See Ezek. ix. 4.   [p] See Ezek. ix. 1—7.

and many thousands of their countrymen had been
carried away captive to Babylon, they themselves must
be special favourites of the Lord God of Israel. They
disparaged their captive brethren and extolled themselves: "The Temple of the Lord, the Temple of
the Lord, the Temple of the Lord" are we [q]. Theirs
was an hypocritical religion of external ceremonies, of
arrogant self-conceit, and vainglorious self-righteousness; joined with censorious and rash judgments of
others; with malignant scorn, bitterness, and strife, and
with supercilious disdain and virulent hate of all who
spake to them the plain truth in homely language, such
as the prophet Jeremiah, calling them to the exercise of
the moral virtues of justice, righteousness, mercy, and
truth, and rebuking them for their neglect of those
virtues, and denouncing God's judgments upon them
for their hypocrisy. They were a barren leafy fig-tree
—a fig-tree rustling in the breeze with luxuriant green
foliage, but bearing no fruit—and therefore to be
blighted and withered by the breath of God; and
Jeremiah represented to them their own corrupt moral
and spiritual condition by a prophetic parable—that
of the two baskets of figs [r]: the bad figs in the
one basket symbolizing *themselves*, Jerusalem and its
people; while the good figs in the other basket were
emblematic of their captive brethren at Chebar, whom
they despised.

The prophet Ezekiel completed the picture. He
beheld the glory of the Lord, enthroned upon the
cherubim, forsaking the Temple of Jerusalem, which
was profaned by the sins of priests, princes, and people.
He saw the glory of the Lord rising aloft and floating [s]

[q] Jer. vii. 4.   [r] Ibid. xxiv. 1—10.
[s] See Ezek. x. 1—22, xi. 22.

away over the east gate of the Temple to the Mount of Olives, and toward the land of Chaldæa [t].

Brethren, these things are profitable to us. They warn us that the true strength and glory of a Church does not consist in the magnificence of its sacred fabrics, nor in the splendour of its religious ritual, but in the hearts and lives of its people. They teach us that the verdict of *Ichabod* may be pronounced over us, and certainly will be, if we do not cherish those inner graces of holiness, gentleness, meekness, love, truth, and peace, without which the most splendid Minsters and most pompous Ceremonial are abominable in the sight of Him Who searcheth the heart, and Who requires the moral, intellectual, and spiritual sacrifice of the whole inner man.

Both Ezekiel and Jeremiah were priests, as well as prophets. As such they had a special reverence for the Temple at Jerusalem and its Ritual, and for all the requirements of the Levitical Law. They cannot be suspected of any bias towards that fanatical Puritanism which disparages outward forms of religion, and resolves all devotion into a mere subjective spiritualism. And therefore the language of these two Hebrew priests and prophets on this subject is more entitled to our attention [u]. The message of Ezekiel to Israel, a message repeated with earnest solemnity [x], was this, "the soul that sinneth it shall die." He declares that though the greatest saints were collected together from the Hagiology of every age, and were concentrated as contemporaries in a Church in one age—"though Noah, Daniel, and Job

[t] Ezek. x. 20—22.
[u] See, for example, Jer. iv. 4, and vii. 22, ix. 25, 26; and on Ezek. xviii. 31, xxxi. 18, xxxii. 19, 20, xxxvi. 26, on the necessity of the true circumcision, the circumcision of the heart.
[x] Ezek. xviii. 4, 20.

were in it [y]—they shall deliver neither sons nor daughters, they shall deliver only their own souls by their righteousness, saith the Lord God."

What is this, brethren, but to teach us that we may not rely for our acceptance with God on the privileges of Church-membership, except so far as we are making those privileges our own by a right use of them, and by bringing forth their fruits in our lives? What is this, but to remind us that each individual soul among us is to be brought singly, one by one, into personal communion and contact with God, and to stand, as it were, confronted, face to face, with Him, and to be left alone with Him, disentangled from all the intertwinings and interweavings of all other souls, and to bear its own burden, and to be placed in independent isolation by its divine Judge, and to be scanned and scrutinized through and through by His divine eye, and to receive its own sentence from Him, for everlasting bliss or woe, at the great Day.

Surely it is an awful thought, and it is made more awful by the view which the prophet presents to us of the sinfulness of sin: "The soul that sinneth it shall die." This is the burden of Ezekiel's prophecy. The practical comment which he gives on these words is full of meaning. Ezekiel at the river Chebar had by divine illumination a vision of the siege of Jerusalem: "Son of man, write the name of the day, even of this same day; the king of Babylon set himself against Jerusalem this same day [z]." Ezekiel had also a prophetic revelation of the miseries of that siege, and of its woeful catastrophe. And soon afterwards, probably on the same day in which Jerusalem was taken, he had another message,—" Son of man, behold I take away from

[y] Ezek. xiv. 14, 20.   [z] Ibid. xxiv. 2.

thee *the desire of thine eyes* with a stroke, yet neither shalt thou mourn nor weep, neither shall thy tears run down." He was forbidden to put on the attire, or utter the lamentations, of a mourner. So (he adds) "I spake unto the people in the morning; and in the evening *my wife died;* and I did in the morning as I was commanded [a]."

The Hebrew captives at Chebar were astounded at such demeanour as this, and asked the reason of it. The prophet answered them that he himself—he, Ezekiel,—was to be a sign to them; and that what he himself did, they must also do. They had hoped for a speedy return to Jerusalem, their own home—their whole hearts were there. Jerusalem was the *desire of their eyes;* it was dear to them as a wife; but Jerusalem was to be suddenly smitten. God would take it away from them by an unexpected death-stroke. In them were to be realized the words, "I spake unto the people: in the evening my wife died." The fall of Jerusalem was the death of their wife. And yet they must not weep nor mourn for its fall [b]. "Ye," says the prophet, "shall do as I have done." They were not to weep or mourn even for the destruction of Sion by the armies of Babylon; but they must mourn and weep for something else. All their tears were to be reserved for *that:* all their sorrow for the destruction of Jerusalem was to be merged and absorbed in sorrow for *that.* And what was it? It was *their own sin*, and the sin of their countrymen; for this it was which caused her fall. Ye shall not mourn nor weep for the destruction of the city and the Temple, dear as they are to you. No; but what does the prophet add? "*But ye shall pine away for your iniquities and mourn one toward another.*"

[a] Ezek. xxiv. 18.   [b] Ibid. xxiv. 21, 22.

Brethren, here is instruction for us all. No sufferings, however great,—not the loss of a dear wife, not the disestablishment of a national Church, not the ruin of a beloved Country, although these things are entwined with all our tenderest affections,—are to draw forth from our eyes a single tear, in comparison with our own sins, which are the real source and well-spring of all our miseries in Church and State. We must pine away for our own iniquities and mourn towards one another.

At this present time we ourselves may be trembling for the safety of our own Sion. And we have cause to do so. Let us therefore look inward. Let us examine our own hearts and own hands. Let us scrutinize our own lives. Let us seek and pray earnestly for grace, that we may feel more deeply the heinousness of our own sins. Let us put away all envy, strife, hatred and malice, and be at one among ourselves. Let us cleanse the sanctuary of our own hearts. Let us cherish the graces of faith and love, truth and peace, kindness and equity, which are its best ornaments—ornaments far more lovely than the sculptured lilies and carved cherubim and palm-trees which decorated the Temple of Solomon. Then God will be with us. Then the glory of the divine Shekinah will not float away from the courts of our Sion to the lonely river of some distant Chebar. And no armies of Babylon will ever be able to destroy the walls, and to profane the Holy Place of the Temple of our Jerusalem.

Once more; whatever in God's providential visitation may be in store for our own Country, and for our own Church—whatever may befall other Nations and other national Churches—Ezekiel, at the river Chebar, provides comfort for the faithful in every age and clime.

The destruction of the city and Temple at Jerusalem was like the death of a beloved wife. It was a sadder pang to them than the death of his dear Rachel to the patriarch Jacob at Bethlehem. The expatriation of the citizens of Jerusalem from that dear, dear home, their dispersion as wanderers and captives in a far-off heathendom, was like a national widowhood and a national orphanhood. But yet the Lord God of Israel was the God of all true Israelites in Chaldæa as well as in Judah. He is the God of every land and every age. He is JEHOVAH ELOHIM. And this great truth was brought out more clearly by the destruction of Jerusalem and its Temple, and by the scattering of her princes, priests, and people into the far-off regions of the East. They learnt thus to realize God's Omnipresence. They learnt that true religion does not depend on the material fabric of a Temple, however glorious; nor on its religious Ritual, however gorgeous, and even though it be prescribed by God Himself; but that it depends on the presence of God in the hearts of His people. The glory of the Lord God had been seen by the prophet Ezekiel riding away in the clouds on the winged chariot of the Cherubim from the Temple of Jerusalem. And why? Because that Temple was profaned by the sins of the worshippers in it. And this migration of the God of the Temple was a signal that He had given it up to destruction. But that glory of the Lord was seen by the prophet in the wilderness of Chaldæa on the banks of the river Chebar, four hundred miles from Jerusalem; and God had said to him, "I will be your Sanctuary [e]."

Thus it was revealed to the world, that though Thrones may totter and fall, though Cities may be thrown pros-

[e] Ezek. xi. 16.

trate on the ground, though Dynasties, Empires, and Kingdoms pass away like visionary shadows and spectral phantoms, though Nations may be scattered, and national Churches may fall, yet there is the same JEHOVAH, —the same Triune God—ever sitting enthroned on the cherubim, ever riding on His winged evangelic chariot of the fourfold Gospel throughout the world; and though we be exiles and prisoners in Chaldæa with Ezekiel, or with St. John at Patmos, yet with them we may have visions of God. And this blessed assurance is confirmed to us by the Holy Spirit speaking to us by Ezekiel, and revealing to us in the last nine chapters[d] of his sublime prophecy the glories of the Church of Christ Universal, which is our indestructible Sion, and summing up all with those memorable words,—"the name of the city from that day shall be JEHOVAH SHAMMAH,"—the LORD is THERE[e].

[d] Ezek. xl.—xlviii.   [e] Ibid. xlviii. 35.

SERMON V.

The Prophet at Bochim.

JUDGES ii. 4.

"And it came to pass, when the angel of the Lord spake these words unto all the children of Israel, that the people lifted up their voice, and wept."

THE Prophet at Bochim! It is perhaps the most wonderful incident in the whole history of prophecy to which your thoughts are to be turned tonight. There are concentrated around this narrative the leading features of all other prophecy; whether we regard the speaker or the listeners, the nature of the message or the manner of its reception, only in a higher and intenser form. "And an angel of the Lord came up from Gilgal to Bochim, and said." The startling abruptness of the beginning of the history is paralleled but scarcely equalled by the suddenness with which the great prophet of an after age is brought before us: "And Elijah the Tishbite, who was of the inhabitants of Gilead, said unto Ahab, As the Lord God of Israel liveth, before whom I stand, there shall not be dew nor rain these years, but according to my word." In both cases there is the same absence of preliminary information as to the person of the witness who suddenly lifts up his voice for God. Out of the thick darkness in either instance he stands before us reproving, warning. We shall see presently that Elijah himself, in all the majesty of his stern mission, in all the loneliness of his separate life, is but a dim shadow of the mightier one of Bochim. It is, however, to be observed in the outset, that this second chapter of the Book of Judges, which commences so abruptly, is to be read in close connection with the first chapter. After the death of Joshua, the Israelites proceeded to go up, it is related, against the Canaanite inhabitants of the land to take possession of their several allotments. Here occurred the first national sin. From various motives—sloth, avarice, eagerness to enter upon the enjoyment of the rich country—they did not thoroughly exterminate the divinely-doomed nations. Judah drave out the inhabitants of the mountain, but could not drive out the inhabitants of the valley. The children of Benjamin did not drive out the Jebusites that inhabited Jerusalem, but the Jebusites dwelt *with* the children of Benjamin. Neither did Manasseh drive out the inhabitants of their lot, but the Canaanites would dwell in that land. And it came to pass, when Israel was strong, that they put the Canaanites to tribute. So with the other tribes; they reduced the original possessors so far as to turn them to their profit by making them tax-payers, and no further. This was a breach of the original covenant with God. In the very opening of their history they wholly lost sight of the supernatural character of their mission as a people, of the repeated charge that they were to enter into no compact with the native races. Stripped of its special accessories, the sin was that of conniving at and patronizing idolatry. And now they are gathered together, probably at Shiloh, for one of the chief religious festivals. Little thought was there in that assembly that in their remissness they had laid the foundation of interminable disasters; we may rather imagine the prevailing temper to have been one of self-gratulation. They had entered on their heritage, they had made good and lucrative conditions of peace with their enemies; they had saved themselves much of toil and suffering by accepting their tribute, instead of pursuing a war of extermination. So tribe passed on to tribe the language of rejoicing, and exulted in the speedy and easy acquisition of the honey-land, when lo, into their midst, unheralded, unforeseen, came one whom they knew not. He counted kindred with none, he claimed not to be priest or prince. Like Melchisedec, he stood before them without father or mother, but a curse on his lips instead of a blessing: he professed not even to speak in the *Name of the Lord*. More than this, as he poured forth against them the tremendous charge of having broken their covenant and forfeited God's promise, he declared *himself* to be their deliverer from Pharaoh, *himself* the giver of the good land. "*I* made you to go up out of Egypt. *I* said *I* will never break my covenant with you. But ye have not obeyed *my* voice." Wherefore I also said, "*I* will not drive them out from before you, but they shall be as thorns in your sides." The conscience of the people at once responded to the rebuke. The true words, the awful assumption of underived authority in the speaker, fell with irresistible force upon the hearts of the assembled multitudes. The arrow went straight to the mark. At once that summer day of mutual congratulation went down in gloom. "And it came to pass, when the angel of the Lord spake these words unto all the children of Israel, that the people lifted up their voice, and wept. And they called the name of that place Bochim," that is, "the place of weepers."

Here is the story, let us examine it closely. And, first, as to the prophet who spake.

I. Now it is to be here observed that the reprover of the people is termed an angel. It need not surprise us to find that, taking the word in the lowest sense, some have understood by it only a prophet sent by God as His messenger. But as Bishop Patrick says, no instance can be given of an ordinary prophet being called an angel of the Lord. If, however, we take the natural and higher sense of the word, another question arises,—Are we to consider the speaker to be one of the heavenly host sent like Gabriel to Daniel? Now there are several things which militate against this. In the Book of Judges are two other recorded visits of an angel, and in both those instances the language is such as to lead us to a higher conception of his nature. Thus we read, "And the *angel of the Lord* appeared unto Gideon;" but a few verses further on it is written, "And the Lord looked upon him." The passage is thus very similar to that which relates that the "angel of the Lord appeared unto Moses in a flame of fire out of the midst of a bush [a]," whilst immediately afterwards it is said "God called unto him out of the midst of the bush." So we read how "Jacob was left alone, and there wrestled a man with him until the breaking of the day [b]." Yet Jacob himself declares that on that wonderful night he had seen "God" face to face. And the prophet Hosea describing the event, says, "He had power over the angel, and prevailed [c];" and in the same verse, "He found him in Bethel, and there he spake with us, even the Lord God of hosts." The man is first described as an angel, and then identified with

[a] Exod. iii. 2.   [b] Gen. xxxii. 24.   [c] Hosea xii. 4.

the Lord of hosts. Again, in this Book of Judges [d], we are told of an angel of the Lord appearing to Manoah and Manoah's wife. And upon Manoah demanding "What is thy name?" the reply is, "Why asketh thou after my name, seeing it is *secret*, or *wonderful*, the very name given by the prophet Isaiah to the Messiah [e]." So with the text. An angel of the Lord came up from Gilgal, but the first utterance carries us to the thought of One higher than angel or archangel. The speaker at once describes Himself as the deliverer of Israel out of Egypt, who had sworn unto them, who had made a covenant with them, and finishes with the denunciation, "Ye have not obeyed *my voice.*" All this is said without the prefixing any such words as, "Thus saith the Lord," which would have been the form if the speaker had spoken in God's Name, and not in his own.

Again, it is to be noted *whence* the angel-preacher is said to have come. "An angel of the Lord came up from Gilgal." Why from Gilgal? Turn to the fifth chapter of Joshua, and you find that it was in the camp at Gilgal that there appeared unto Joshua the mysterious vision of the armed man, who described himself as captain of the host of the Lord, i.e. leader or prince of the angelic hierarchy, whose presence, like the Presence in the burning bush, made the very soil around Him holy. The coming up from Gilgal seems to connect at once the prophet of Bochim with the vision of Joshua. And the vision of Joshua again links itself with the appearance to Moses in the bush. To what, then, does all this tend? Why to the conclusion that in these places, and in many others, we have a previous manifestation of the second Person in

[d] Judges xiii.   [e] Compare Bishop Patrick *in loco.*

the Trinity in the *form* of that *manhood* which in the latter days He was about to take into God. The Old Testament is full of these pre-revelations. They are the visible, bodily exhibitions of the truth conveyed in the words, "Behold, I send an angel before thee to keep thee in the way. Beware of him, and obey his voice ; do not rebel against him, for he will not pardon your transgressions, for My Name is in him." The angel is here invested with the whole majesty of God. In other passages he is called the Angel of the Presence,—The face of God, (what is this but in St. Paul's language the "express image of God?") *the* angel of the Lord, the angel which redeemeth from all evil. There is, if we may so say, a wonderful symmetry and harmony in the passages thus interpreted. They are a marvellous witness to the unity of the Bible. We see *one truth* pervading the whole framework of inspiration, *one* thought ever kept before the minds of the devout, to be consummated in the fulness of time. "God made Man."

But if we thus identify the angel at Bochim with the angel of the covenant, the eternal Word or Logos, then have we here a very remarkable pre-manifestation of him in one of his *three* great offices, viz. that of *prophet or teacher*. We must here recall to our minds the moral element of prophecy. Popularly a prophet is one who foretells future events, but this is a very partial conception of the office of the old prophets of Israel. Primarily the prophets were men raised up by God to enforce the *moral* law upon the national conscience, and to carry out further than the law of Moses had done the revelation of God's attributes, and the relations of man to Him and to the Eternal Word. It is not that the ancient prophets stood forth to foretell things to come, and occasionally intermingled their predictions with lessons of holiness. The converse is rather the fact. The prophet was inspired to arouse and waken the hearts of the people, and he was occasionally enabled to enforce his religious teaching by unfolding the roll of coming events.

So it has been said the prophets of Israel occupy a middle position between the Law and the Gospel; rising above the former in their disclosures of the life everlasting, of the spirituality of the divine nature, of the principles of personal holiness, but falling short of the latter in its complete unveiling of the mystery of godliness.

"The prophets," says Bishop Horsley, "spake under the influence of the Spirit when they had no predictions of the future to deliver." They were the ordinary preachers of righteousness. The mind of the prophet seems to have been very differently affected with these moral subjects, and with the visions of futurity. The counsel he was to give was presented naked, without the disguise of imagery, to his thoughts, and he gave it utterance in perspicuous phrases, carrying a definite and obvious meaning. The whole mission of Elijah is an instance of this. His greatness consists not in the clearness of his predictions of distant events, but in the force with which he withstood Ahab and stemmed the tide of idolatry.

And of this great company of the reprovers of national sin from generation to generation, we have the shadow cast before at Bochim. The mysterious Being unto whom all the prophets bare witness, in whose teaching with authority the profoundest verities of God all their teaching was to be consummated, appears before the gathered thousands of Israel at the outset of their career, Himself face to face the Rebuker of their sin; Himself as it were setting the note of that great anthem of prophecy, whose majestic strains were to follow age after age the generations of His people until, not in the semblance of man, but verily made man, He should teach daily in the Temple. And the burden of the prophecy at Bochim is worthy of the divine speaker, for it is the simple enunciation of the foundation truth of all religion, "Man in covenant with God," bound to comply with the terms of the covenant, even when, like the extermination of the Canaanite tribes, passing his understanding to account for. It was no message of temporary interest with which the angel-preacher stood before the people. The whole germ of revealed religion was in his words. "The goodly fellowship of the prophets praise thee, oh Christ,"—All the after-utterances of that great confraternity were but the prolonged echo of the prophesying at Bochim. Elijah at the mouth of the cave, Jeremiah beholding in the spirit the shattered ruins of Jerusalem, Ezekiel in the land of his exile, did but bewail the same broken compact which formed the burden of the first prophetic cry which fell like a voice from heaven upon the astonished multitude, when the angel of the covenant stood among them in the plain of Bochim.

II. And now we turn for a few minutes to the result of this prophesying. "And it came to pass, when the angel of the Lord spake these words unto all the children of Israel, that the people lifted up their voice, and wept. And they called the name of that place Bochim: and they sacrificed there unto the Lord." If the angel-prophet is a manifestation of Christ Jesus as the great prophet of the Church, so that we have in his reproving the people at Bochim a type of one of His perpetual offices, so in the result of that reproof have we a representation of the general effect of the prophetic mission. Doubtless individual Israelites in that vast assembly were touched with the words of their reprover; doubtless as they heard him bring out clearly the fact of the covenant of God broken by their sloth and avarice, some sorrowed with a sorrow unto salvation, and souls were recovered from the snare, and the light of devotion rekindled in many a household. Yet the *general* result was but transitory. "The people lifted up their voices and wept," and they sacrificed unto the Lord. But no amendment ensued. There was no forsaking their ease, no turning with fresh courage to the sacred warfare with the Canaanite, no loosing the league with the idolaters. The next verses tell us of the Israelites themselves "serving Baalim," "forsaking the God of their fathers," "worshipping Ashtaroth." The whole effect was a momentary outburst of feeling, and a hasty sacrifice. Most true picture of the reception of God's Word in after times!

"They lifted up their voice and wept." It is sensational or emotional religion against which Bochim is our warning. There is in every soul not hardened by a long course of sin an instinctive sense of truth, which echoes the remonstrances of God's messenger; a chord which vibrates at once to the breath of the Divine Word. This instinctive appreciation of truth shewed itself in the impulsive Eastern nature by an out-break of tears; it shews itself amongst ourselves in analogous ways, but equally profitless and vain. As the solemn utterances of God's truth drop upon the ear, and the weighty words of one whom God has gifted with persuasive power force home the reality of wasted energies and lost opportunities, there is often awakened in the listener a keen sorrow, flowing (it may be) out of regret —regret for loss of character and influence ; a sense of increasing loneliness as this life is felt to be ebbing, and no foundation laid for the next ; a sad remembrance of earlier years, in their purity and freshness, when the covenant with God was unbroken. He will go away from the church, sobered, saddened, depressed, and yet in how many instances no change of life ensues. There is no resolute amendment of evil habits. The man will seem to himself even to have been religiously impressed, yet indeed there may have been no true religion in what he has experienced. The sorrow ending in itself is but the weeping of Bochim ; a sorrow that, by misleading, worketh only death.

There are two principal elements of this fruitless sorrow : the first is *want of depth of soul.* There are hearts which answer readily to every movement, be it glad or painful, selfish or generous, yet never retain any impression, but pass with a revolting fickleness from one extreme to another; "Because it had no deepness of earth it withered away." It is our Lord's own description of the fate of the good seed sown in those men of shallow soul.

A second element of the transitiveness of such half-religious impressions is the "after revolt of the human mind against the supernatural." When the angel-prophet stood suddenly in the midst of the gathered Israel, and poured forth the burning rebuke for a broken covenant, for awhile the hearts of the people bowed before him. "Just as in the garden of Gethsemane, when those who came forth with swords and staves to take our Lord first saw Him, they went backward and fell to the ground," and yet immediately after they laid hands upon Him. So was it at Bochim. In either case there was, we may believe, an ineffable majesty, a shadow of deity, unseen but felt about the Divine Being, which for an instant subdued all to itself. But very soon the mind, which is so elastic under the heaviest burden, roused itself against the true impulse, and fell back to its own purpose of evil. As the last words of the unknown prophet died upon the hushed air, and he departed into the mystery out of which he had come, the heart of the people was broken. Then after awhile they doubtless asked themselves, "Was there really anything supernatural in it? was it not only some mad fellow who had assumed the tone of an inhabitant of heaven?" It is ever so. "If another, said our Lord, should come in his own name, him ye will receive." Talk to many a man about virtue on the grounds of worldly interest, philosophy, moral dignity, and you may get a hearing; found your argument upon the Revelation of God in Christ, claim to have a message from heaven to earth, and the same listener will question and doubt and cavil. Hence, again, the fruitlessness so often of religious emotion. The heart for a moment quails under the sword of the Spirit. Then comes the after-recoil against the supernatural claim, and the sorrow proves the sorrow of Bochim, giving birth to nothing. *And they offered sacrifice to the Lord.* Yes, here was one issue of that national weeping. Not *amendment*, but *a burnt-offering*. What have we here again but the type of that emotional piety which is not strong enough to produce a turning away from sin, but satisfies itself with a few devotional practices, a prayer repeated, it may be, with some additional fervour; a sacrament received with a little more attention, and then goes back to the old habit of idleness, or profligacy, having added only to its list of offences another quenching of the Spirit of Grace.

Would God, men and brethren, as we look back through the dimness of 3,000 years to that plain of the weepers, and hear, as it were, the prolonged Eastern wail which follows the retiring steps of the angel-prophet, and mark the uprising smoke of the sacrifice, and then see that whole multitude, recovering from their transitory awe, and instead of going forth with renewed ardour to battle with the Canaanite, subsiding into their former apathy and ease, aye, sinking into the profounder depth of utter apostacy, that we might take alarm at the religious feeling which is awakened only to sleep again, at the piety which says, "I go, Sir," but goes not, contenting itself with its own tears, whilst shrinking from the warfare of Christ.

The plain of the weepers! Every age of the Church has its Bochim. Every place has it in a greater or less degree. Susceptibility of emotion varies infinitely. It varies according to physical constitution, or nervous temperament, according to peculiarities of race or manners. Hence is it no test of godly sorrow, which is one and the same, like the nature of God Himself. And this is its great characteristic. Godly sorrow issues in *a repentance not to be repented of;* in that thorough turning of the life to God's service, from which, in the hottest fire of temptation, there is never a turning back to the way of evil again.

SERMON VI.

Isaiah.

ISAIAH vi. 8—10.

"I heard the voice of the Lord, saying, Whom shall I send, and who will go for us? Then said I, Here am I; send me. And He said, Go, and tell this people, Hear ye indeed, but understand not; and see ye indeed, but perceive not. Make the heart of this people fat, and make their ears heavy, and shut their eyes; lest they see with their eyes, and hear with their ears, and understand with their heart, and convert, and be healed."

SUCH was the heavy burden laid upon Isaiah in his fresh youth, probably at much your age. Like St. Paul—he had seen the glory of God; he had seen, as man could in the flesh see and live, God Himself; he had witnessed the burning love of those fiery spirits of love, the Seraphim; he had felt, in that awful Presence of the All-Holy, the sinfulness of man and his own. Holy and pure he must have been; for even in that dread Presence, while shrinking abashed into himself as "undone," from his unfitness to behold It, nothing flashes into his mind, even in that all-revealing light, no spot of sin is visible to him in his God-enlightened memory, except some *words*. "Woe is me, for I am a man of unclean lips." Sins of words, as well as sins of deeds, were one wide offence of his people. He had, in his prophetic office, often to warn against them. But a national sin is infectious. Individuals partake of it more or less, at least in its lighter shades, because it *is* the national character. It is, perhaps, the last to be extirpated. For an impatient, God-unhonouring not God-dishonouring, word, Moses had lost the hope of those fourscore years, that he should bring his people into the land which God had promised them. "By thy words shalt thou be justified," says our Lord, "and by thy words shalt thou be condemned." Isaiah did not excuse himself, that they were *only* words. The words (not such as men now think nothing of), whether they were of impatience, or untempered zeal, or harsh reproof, or whatever they were, rose in his soul, and called out the penitential cry, "Woe is me! for I am undone; because I am a man of unclean lips, and I dwell in the midst of a people of unclean lips: for mine eyes have seen the King, the Lord of Hosts." Perhaps God, as He often does in those whom He early calls, had awakened in him the longing to speak to his God-forgetting people in the Name of God. Perhaps, as God had awakened in Moses, while yet in Pharaoh's court, the consciousness that he was to be God's instrument in delivering his people, and had so filled his soul with the thought, that he wondered that they understood not the meaning of his slaying the Egyptian; so He had kindled in Isaiah the burning longing to be employed by God to His degenerate people. God discloses Himself to the hearts which He has prepared. And now at the sight of God, he felt how all-unfit he was to speak in the Name of the All-Holy God. "Woe is me! for I am undone." His longing must have lived, if he could but be fitted for the mission which he longed for. But the sight of God had pierced his soul with the conviction, how holy His words must be, because they are the words of the All-Holy; how holy ought to be the lips which would take those words upon them; how pure *he* should be, who would be the messenger of God the All-Holy to sinful man. Job defended himself long against the unjust inferences of his friends from his miseries. When God revealed Himself to him, he said, "I heard of Thee by the hearing of the ear, but now mine eye seeth Thee; wherefore I abhor myself, and repent in dust and ashes." And now, like him, Isaiah is as one dead. The sentence, which guilty man of himself deserves from the Holy God, was, already in his feeling, fulfilled on him, "I am cut off." Then followed that wondrous type, of the Incarnation first and then of the Holy Eucharist, the living heavenly Fire in a visible form, the Coal from the Altar; and that, which the incorporeal Seraph out of reverence touched not, was approached to his lips, the type of Him "by Whom the guilt of the world is purged [a]." "This has touched thy lips, and thine iniquity is gone, thy sin is atoned for." And then God, the Holy Trinity,—Whose praises he had heard, sung by the Seraphim in their Trisagion, which the Church has caught up from them,—willing that he should have the reward of a spontaneous self-oblation, elicit in words the devotion which They had inspired, and ask, "Whom shall I send, and who will go for Us?" And Isaiah summed up his whole future life in those two words [b], "Behold me; send me." Then on his ardent soul was poured the heavy message, "Go, and thou shalt tell *this* people," (God speaks of them no more as His own,) "Hear ye on, and understand not; and see ye on, and know not. Make thou dull the heart of this people, and its ears make thou heavy, and its eyes close thou; lest it see with its eyes, and with its ears hearken, and its heart understand, and it return and one heal it."

[a] See passages of Fathers in "Doctrine of the Real Presence," pp. 119 sqq.   [b] הנני שלחני.

Startling office for one so sanguine and so young! heavy burden to bear for probably sixty-one years of life, to be closed by a martyr's excruciating death! Outside of that commission there was hope; hope, because the promises of God could not fail of fulfilment; hope, because in the worst times of Israel there had been those seven thousand which the Prophet knew not of, but of whom God revealed to him, who had stood faithful to God amid the national apostacy; hope, because when God pronounces not a doom, we may take refuge in the loving mercy of Him Who swears by Himself, "As I live, saith the Lord God, I have no pleasure in the death of the wicked, but," (the "but" says, "in *this* I have pleasure," on this Almighty God dwells with pleasure,) "in the turning of the wicked from his way, and that he live; turn ye, turn ye from your evil ways; for why will ye die, O house of Israel c?"

The message was to the people, not to individuals: "Go ye to this people, and say." It related to individuals, only as they were such as the mass of the nation was, as they themselves made up that mass. But a burning zeal enters into the mind of God, Who "willeth that all men should be saved, and should come to the knowledge of the truth d." A burning love entered into the mind of Him, in thought of Whom Isaiah found his solace, "Who died for all e." Yet we know how St. Paul f attests, "my conscience bearing me witness in the Holy Ghost, that I have great grief and unintermitting sorrow in my heart," so that he could wish even to be severed from the Presence of Christ, never to behold Him Who had died for him, in Whom was his life, Who was his life within him, if so be Israel might be saved. And now

---

c Ezek. xxxiii. 11. d 1 Tim. ii. 2. e 2 Cor. v. 14.
f Rom. ix. 1.

this, in all seeming, was the thankless office to which Isaiah was called, to be heard, to be listened to, by some with contempt, by others with seeming respect, and to leave things in the main worse than he found them. Even with our little love, we know what heaviness it is, to pass along any of our crowded places of concourse, in the streets of any of those centres of human activity, and to see undying souls, with their master-passions impressed upon their countenances, living for the world, and not for God. But they have their own one talent, whatever it may be: their souls may, we trust, be saved. Isaiah's commission was far harder, to act towards a loveless faith. His office was towards those, in part at least, who were ever-hearing, never-doing, and so never understanding. And so, (so to speak,) he was only to make things worse. So St. Paul says [g], "The earth which drinketh in the rain which cometh oft upon it—if it bring forth thorns and briars, is accounted worthless and nigh unto cursing," not yet accursed, (thanks be to God,) yet nigh unto it, "whose end," if it remains such unto the end, " is to be burned." There were better among the people; there were worse; but such was the general character; it was an ever-hearing,—hearing,—hearing (such is the force of the words, "hear ye hearing on [h]," evermore,) never wearied of hearing, yet never doing; ever seeing as they thought, yet never gaining insight, and so becoming ever duller, their sight ever more and more bleared, until to hear and to see would become well-nigh and to man impossible. The more they heard and saw, the further they were from understanding, from being converted, from healing reaching to them. Such they were, God says, a little later, in Ezekiel's time. You know how they

[g] Heb. vi. 7, 8.   [h] שִׁמְעוּ שָׁמוֹעַ.

came to the prophet of God, but had set up every man his idol in his heart, (who was indeed his god,) and how God says, "Are ye come to enquire of Me? As I live, saith the Lord God, I will not be enquired of by you [1]." Nay, so coming, they should only be the more deceived. And of this Isaiah was to be the occasion and the instrument. So it was when *He* came, of Whom Isaiah prophesied. They thought that they knew the law, but only to allege their interpretation of it against Him. The more they heard, the more they were blinded. And their imagined seeing and their real blindness, was their condemnation. "If ye were blind," our Lord says, "ye should not have sin; but now ye say, We see, therefore your sin remaineth [j]." This is inseparable from every revelation of God, from every preaching of the Gospel, from every speaking of God inwardly to the soul, from every motion of God the Holy Ghost, every drawing or forbidding of that judge which He has placed within, our conscience, every hearing of God's Word. All and each leave the soul in a better condition or a worse. Not by any direct hardening from God, not through any agency of the Prophet, but by man's free-will, hearing but not obeying, seeing but not doing, feeling but resisting, the preaching of the Prophet would leave them only more hopelessly far from conversion, that God might heal them.

And what said the Prophet? Contrary as the sentence must have been to all the yearnings of his soul, crushing to his hopes, he knew that it must be just, because "the Judge of the whole world" "must do right [k]." He intercedes, but only by those three words, "Lord, how long?" He appeals to God. Such could not be God's ultimate purpose with His people; not for this could

---
[1] Ezek. xx. 3.   [j] St. John ix. 41.   [k] Gen. xviii. 25.

He have taken them out of all nations to be a peculiar people to Himself. The night was to come; sin deserved it; but was it to have no dawn? Hope there is yet, but meanwhile a still-deepening night, a climax of woe; and that in two stages. In the first, "cities left without inhabitants;" and not cities only, as a whole, but "houses too tenantless;" nor these alone, but "the whole land desolate, and God removes the inhabitants far away, and there shall be a great forsaking in the midst of the land." Nor this only, but when, in this sifting-time, nine parts should be gone, and one-tenth only remain, this should be again consumed: only, like those trees which survived the winters and storms of a thousand years, while the glory wherewith God once clad it was gone, its hewn stem was still to live; "a holy seed" was to be the stock thereof.

The vision, opened before him, stretches on until now and to the end. His question, "How long? Until when?" implied a hope that there would be an end; the answer "until," declared that there would be an end. We have, in one, that first carrying away, the small remnant which should return; its new desolation; the holy seed which should survive; the restoration at the end, of which St. Paul says, then "all Israel shall be saved[1]."

And this message fell on one of the tenderest of hearts in its early freshness. As he is eminently the Gospel-prophet, the Evangelist in the old covenant, so he had already been taught by the Holy Ghost the Gospel-lesson, "Love your enemies." He denounces God's judgments; but, himself the type of Him who wept over Jerusalem, "My heart," he says, "shall cry out from Moab[m]," who was ever banded against his people. "I will water thee with my tears, O Heshbon;

[1] Rom. xi. 26.   [m] Isa. xv. 5, xvi. 9, 11.

my bowels shall sound like a harp for Moab, and my inward parts for Kir-haresh." Even Babylon, whom he foreknew as God's appointed waster of His people, the world-power who should uproot His people, and carry them far away, even Babylon moved him in its fall. Present in spirit at a doom which was to come nearly two centuries later, he was himself in spirit as one of the sufferers. "My loins," he says, "are filled with reeling cramp; writhing pangs have laid hold of me, as the pangs of a woman in travail. I am bowed down, that I cannot hear; I am terror-stricken, that I cannot see. My heart reeleth; horror hath terrified me: the eventide of my desire hath He made into terror to me[n]." If Isaiah so felt for the destroyer of his people, was so horror-stricken for the woes of those yet unborn, what for *their* sufferings who were flesh of his flesh and bone of his bone, whose woes he had to tell them, face to face, and which would come upon them because they would not hear! O what a woe it is, to see certainly before one those judgment-fires, into which people are rushing madly, because they will not believe them or look at them!

And in this his general grief for his people, there were so many particular griefs, as many as there were forms of evil. All confronted him. For his office lay in the heart of the material prosperity, the intellect, the corruptions, the rebellions, the oppressions of his people, the city of David[o], once "the faithful, now the harlot-city, where righteousness once dwelt, and now murderers[p]." There, in Jotham's sixteen years, there was all the insolence of human pride, "high and lifted up[q];" in Uzziah's next sixteen years the whole weight of the king's authority was thrown in against the faith, from

[n] Isa. xxi. 3, 4.   [o] Ibid. xxix. 1   [p] Ibid. i. 21.   [q] Ibid. ii. 6, 7.

his first scarce-veiled insolence in rejecting the prophet's offer in the name of God to give him what sign he would of the verity of his promise in his trouble, to his naked apostacy, when he closed the Temple, suspended its worship, burned his sons in the dreadful worship of Moloch, made every corner of Jerusalem a shrine of idolatry, and desecrated every city by its own idol-chapel[r]. Then came Hezekiah's reformation, in himself personally devout, but powerless over his people; the thickening troubles of his country, unconverted by each successive scourge. "The people turneth not to Him that smiteth them, neither do they seek the Lord of Hosts[s]." And so his burden still had to be, "For all this His anger is not turned away, but His Hand is stretched out still[t]." Under Manasseh, the tide of evil, which Hezekiah's personal influence had stayed, burst out uncontrolled; it swept along with it the boy-king of twelve years also, thereafter himself to give fresh impulse to the current, to flood Jerusalem with monstrosities of cruelty and lust, as worship of their gods[u], and, (too late for his land though not for his soul,) to turn to God. Martyrdom crowns those only who resist. In witnessing then for God, though in this reign he uttered no recorded prophecy, God, after his threescore years of service, ordered that he should close his life's long martyrdom with a martyr's death. Strange likeness to our Lord, of Whom he spake so much, if, in that reign of terror and of blood, occasion was found for slaying him through distortion of his words[x]!

This great outline of suffering was filled up variedly. Ahaz' scornful rejection echoed on in the unbelieving

---

[r] 2 Chron. xxviii. 2, 3, 23—25.   [s] Isa. ix. 13.   [t] Ibid. xii. 17, 21.
[u] 2 Kings xxi.; 2 Chron. xxxiii. 2—6.   [x] See Yebamoth, iv. fin., quoted by Martini, Pug. fid., f. 700, (p. 899, 900, Carpz.)

taunts of the great or the learned. They ridiculed the simplicity of his teaching. It was but fit for babes; they were men, and had outgrown it! "line on line, rule on rule; a little here, a little there. Whom should he teach knowledge?" They challenged the Almighty to fulfil His prophet's threats: "Let Him make speed, hasten His work, that we may see; and let the counsel of the Holy One of Israel draw nigh and come, that we may know it!"

> "Bricks fell, hewn stone will we build ;
> Sycomores are hewn down, cedars will we replace¹."

Present judgments, they said, they would more than recover; against threatened judgments they had made their covenant with death, and their agreement with hell [a]; if imminent, they looked to strengthen themselves with human help, not to their Maker [b]; if inevitable, they would enjoy themselves to the end; it was, "Eat, drink, and to-morrow die [c]." The leaders misled [d], the judges judged unjustly [e], the rich left no space for the poor [f], their women had lost modesty [g], their men were oppressors [h]; evil they called good, good evil [i]; chastisement but engendered increased rebellion [k]; the whole head was sick and the whole heart faint [k].

Isaiah could but weep for those who wept not for themselves. "I will be bitter in my weeping," he says; "press not on me to comfort me for the desolation of the daughter of my people¹."

Yet where there is desolation for the sake of God, there is also consolation. Wherein was Isaiah's? Not in the solace of his married life. His daily dress was

---

y Isa. xxviii. 9, 10.   ᶻ Ibid. ix. 10.   a Ibid. xxviii. 15.   b Ibid. xxii. 9—11.   c Ibid. 13.   d Ibid. ix. 16.   e Ibid. i. 17, 23; v. 23.   f Ibid. v. 8.   g Ibid. iii. 16 sq.   h Ibid. iii. 5, 12.   i Ibid. v. 20.   k Ibid. i. 5.   l Ibid. xxii. 4.

like John Baptist's, the hair-cloth pressing upon his loins, wearing to the naked flesh, although mentioned only when he was to put it off and himself to become a portent to his people, walking naked and barefoot[m]. His two sons were, by their names, the continual pictures of that woe on his people; the one spoke only of "the speed of the prey, the haste of the spoil[n]," the other was that sad dirge which so echoes through the Prophets, "a remnant shall return[o]," a remnant only of that people who were to be as the sand of the sea, the stars of heaven[p]. What, then, was his solace?

St. John tells us, in connection with that heavy message, "These things said Isaiah, when he saw His glory and spake of Him[q]." Of whom? Of Christ, of Whom St. John was speaking. Isaiah had seen, as man can see, His Deity. He had seen Him, the Brightness of the Father's Glory and the express Image of His Person; yet he had not seen the Son Alone. He himself says, "Mine eyes have seen Him Who Is, the Lord of Hosts." And the Holy Ghost says by St. Paul, that He spake by Isaiah in these words: "Well said the Holy Ghost by Esaias the Prophet unto our fathers, saying, Go unto this people and say, Hearing, ye shall hear, and shall not understand[r]." Isaiah had not yet the Beatific Vision: "No man hath seen God at any time[s]." Yet he says, "Mine eyes have seen the Lord of Hosts." Not with his bodily eyes did he behold God, nor with his bodily ears did he hear His words, but to his inward sight did God disclose some likeness, whereby he should understand the nature of the Divine Essence, how God, Father, Son, and Holy Ghost, in-

---

[m] Isaiah xx. 2.   [n] Ibid. viii. 3.   [o] Ibid. vii. 3; x. 21.
[p] Gen. xv. 5; xxii. 7.   [q] St. John xii. 41.   [r] Acts xxvi. 25, 26.
[s] St. John i. 18.

exists in Himself, although the Beatific Vision, as He Is, was reserved for the life to come. He had, in his inmost being, in some way, unimaginable to us who have not beheld it, seen the Holy Trinity in Their Unity of Essence, and *that* in the Person of the Son Who said of Himself, "He that hath seen Me, hath seen the Father^t." For It was a Human Form which he beheld, sitting enthroned as the Judge, and receiving the worship of the glowing love of the Seraphim. He had seen Him in His own glory and the glory of the Father, transfiguring the likeness of that Human Form, Which is now, with the Father, the light of Heaven; Which, amid the Uncreated Light which God Is, illumines Heaven also with an Uncreated Light, (as St. John says, "The Lamb is the Light thereof^u,") because "in Him dwelleth all the fulness of the Godhead bodily^x."

How should not this Vision live in him for those threescore years, who knew that thereafter, not through some created image, not by similitude, but face to Face he should behold the End of our being, God? So God prepared him to be,—above all others even of those God-inspired men, those men of zeal and longing and love, "the goodly company of the Prophets"—the Evangelic Prophet, in that he had seen the glory of the Lord.

God's Word is consistent with itself. We need not marvel (as some have done) that he should speak so plainly as he does, that that Child to be born to us was to be "the Mighty God, the Everlasting Lord ^y," or that the Virgin's Son should be called "Immanuel^z," when he had himself seen a Human Form in the ineffable Glory of God. No wonder that he should speak of

---

^t St. John xiv. 9. ^u Rev. xxi. 23. ^x Col. ii. 9.
^y Isa. ix. 6. ^z Ibid. vii. 4; viii. 8.

Him Whom he had seen enthroned as Judge, smiting the earth with the rod of His mouth, and with the breath of His lips slaying the wicked.

This, then, is ever his consolation; this his joy in trouble; this his life in death. The surges of this world, higher and higher as they rose, only bore his soul upward toward his God. He, too, was a man of longing. In the darkness of the world God ever brings this light before him; his darkest visions are the dawn-streaks of the brightest light. Does he describe darkness the image of that outer darkness[a]? Then follows, "The people that walked in darkness have seen a great light." Has he to denounce the utter desolation of all the pride and glory and luxury of the mighty and the beautiful? "Zion, clean-emptied, shall sit on the ground." God teaches him straightway to add, "In that day shall the Branch of the Lord be beauty and glory[b]." And then follow the holiness and peace which He would bestow. Has he to say that the refuge of lies, under which the scornful hoped to hide themselves, shall be swept away? He first says, in the Name of God, "Behold, I lay in Zion for a foundation a Corner-stone, a tried stone, a precious corner-stone: he that believeth shall not haste[c]." Has he to denounce woe on all the houses of joy, in the joyous city[d]? It is but "until the Spirit be poured out from on high," "and the wilderness shall be a fruitful field, and the work of righteousness shall be peace, and the fruit of righteousness quietness and assurance for ever[e]." Has he to speak of the house of David as the stump of a tree hewed down to the ground? "From that hewn stump of Jesse," he says, "there shall come forth a rod, and a Branch shall grow out of his roots, and the Spirit

---

[a] Comp. Isa. viii. 22 with ix. 1. [b] Ibid. iii. 16—26; iv. 2.
[c] Ibid. xxviii. 16—18. [d] Ibid. xxxii. 13. [e] Ibid. 15—17.

of God shall rest upon Him [f];" and then follow the peaceful and peace-giving glories of His reign, and the restoration of the remnant of His people. Has he to tell, how in the captivity of Babylon "they that rule over them make them to howl, and Thy Name every day is blasphemed?" Forthwith he bursts into a jubilee of joy: "How beautiful upon the mountains are the feet of him that bringeth good tidings, that publisheth peace, that bringeth good tidings of good, that publisheth salvation, that saith unto Zion, Thy God reigneth [g]."

Never does that sad message part from his sight. He is like our own loved poet,—

> "Ready to give thanks and live
> On the least that Heaven may give."

He does not live in a bright, ideal future, in Messianic hopes, as men tell you of. His future is as his present, until "death shall be swallowed up in victory." It is still "the remnant shall return; the remnant," he repeats, "shall return to the Mighty God [h];" they are "the gleaning-grapes left in it; as the shaking of an olive-tree, two or three berries in the top of the uppermost bough, four or five in the outmost fruitful branches thereof, saith the Lord God of Israel [i];" "the shaking of an olive-tree, as the gleaning-grapes when the vintage is done [k]." It is what we see before our eyes now, "Ye shall be gathered one by one, O ye children of Israel [l]." And when the Messiah came, it was to be so still. He was to be at once "a sanctuary, but for a stone of stumbling and a rock of offence to both the houses of Israel. And many among them shall stumble, and fall, and be broken, and be snared, and be taken [m]." The words of the aged

---

[f] Isa. xi. 1.   [g] Ibid. lii. 5, 7.   [h] Ibid. x. 21.   [i] Ibid. xvii. 6.
[k] Ibid. xxiv. 13.   [l] Ibid. xxvii. 12.   [m] Ibid. viii. 14.

Simeon but summed up the prophecies of Isaiah: "This Child is set for the fall and rising again of many in Israel, and for a sign which shall be spoken against, that the thoughts of many hearts may be revealed[n]." For such as they were, such did Christ become to them, for the fall of the proud and self-satisfied, for the rising again of those who owned themselves fallen. So Jesus Himself said, "For judgment I am come into this world, that they which see not might see, and that they which see might be made blind[o]."

And so his soul was prepared for that great paradox of prophecy which God revealed through him, the way of whose accomplishment, St. Peter says, was a mystery to them, whose meaning they searched into—the "sufferings of Christ, and the glory which should follow[p]." He, as no other, spake of the buffeting, the spitting upon, the malefactor's death, the counting with the transgressors, the contempt, the constant companionship with grief[q]. He, as few did, spake of the glorious reign, the everlasting rule; how He should reign in righteousness, and be a hiding-place from the storm to those who seek Him, the shadow of a great Rock in this weary and dry land of our banishment from Him. For these should the message for his people be repealed: "The eyes of them that see shall not be dim, and the ears of them that hear shall hearken[r]."

In this hope and longing he lived, in a future for himself, a future which God had promised to the remnant of his people. He was a man of longing: "In the way of Thy judgments have I awaited Thee, O Lord; to Thy Name and Thy memorial is the longing of my soul. With my soul have I longed for Thee in the night; yea,

---

[n] St. Luke ii. 34, 35.   [o] St. John ix. 39.   [p] I St. Peter i. 11.
[q] Isa. l. 6; liii.   [r] Ibid. xxxii. 3.

with my spirit within me I will seek Thee early[s];" "This is our God, we have waited for Him, and He will save us; this is the Lord, we have waited for Him, we will rejoice and be glad in His salvation[t];" "Thou wilt keep him in perfect peace, whose mind is stayed in Thee, for on Thee is it rested[u]." For he looked on beyond this world of disappointment and of shadows. He longed to see Him Who had at the beginning revealed Himself to him, the King on His Throne. "Thine eyes," he says, "shall see the King in His beauty[v]." The grave was to him but a chamber where he should hide himself for a little while[x]; then, to behold what "ear hath not perceived nor eye seen, O God, beside Thee, what He hath prepared for him who waiteth for Him[y]." For for Him had his whole life been one long waiting, and He Himself is the everlasting bliss of those who wait for Him.

Every time has its own pressure in this world of trial. And since we feel most what presses on ourselves, each time seems to those who live in it a time of special trial. Sixteen centuries ago it seemed as if the world was reaching its old age[z]. It attests, they said, its own ruin in the tottering state of things. The time of Antichrist seemed to be approaching[a]; faith seemed to be in a declining or almost slumbering state; priests were wanting in religious devotedness, ministers in entireness of faith; there was no mercy in works, no discipline in manners; modesty was violated in both sexes; the world was renounced in words, not in deeds; men were eager about property and their gains[b], sought to exalt themselves; gave themselves up to emulation and

[s] Isa. xxvi. 8, 9. [t] Ibid. xxv. 9. [u] Ibid. xxvi. 3. [v] Ibid. xxxiii. 17. [x] Ibid. xxvi. 19, 20. [y] Ibid. lxiv. 4 (3 Heb.) [z] S. Cypr. ad Demetr., Oxf. Tr., n. 2, p. 200. [a] Id. ad Fortun. de Martyr. Pref., p. 278. [b] Id., Ep. xi. p. 24.

dissension, were careless about single-mindedness and the faith; they were sundered by unabating quarrels; bishops were engaged in secular vocations, relinquished their chairs, deserted their people, hunted the markets for mercantile profits [c].

But for this last trait, one might think that the Martyr-Bishop of the third century was describing our own times in the nineteenth. Sore as moral and religious evil are, because of that horrible risk of human souls, the Gospel (which is impossible) would be false if they existed not. The presence of unbelief and of moral evil is a confirmation of faith. "Now I have told you, before it comes to pass," our Lord says of men's rejection of Him, "that when it is come to pass, ye may believe [d]."

This chequered aspect of good and ill is but what the Prophets, what our Lord, forewarned us of: it does but verify to us His knowledge of the human heart. Only all good is evidence of His power; the evil is evidence, not of His weakness but of ours. All evil is natural, all good is supernatural. Vice, selfishness, crime, impurity, ambition, covetousness, unbelief, are but the natural growth of the human heart. Faith, self-denial, chastity, content, lowliness, meekness, charity, are supernatural, the working of the Spirit of God. Start not back, then, as if some strange thing had happened, if iniquity abound, if faith seems rare, if zeal looks chilled or wellnigh extinct, if high aims or devotedness lie hid, if a low standard seem to have supplanted the measure of Christ. All this is but of nature. What should we look for in what is mere nature but the works of a corrupt nature, or from the flesh but the works of the flesh, of which the Apostle tells us? The Gospel, and the grace of God in it, has to lift us above nature. And it does. But

[c] Id. de lapsis Treatises, p. 156, O. T.   [d] St. John xiv. 29.

God respects the free-will of the creature which He made in His own Image; He will not destroy what is essential to our likeness to Himself. He will lift us above nature, but only if we, by our God-enfreed will, will it. In our mixed selves, we are evidences at once of the fall and of the restoration. We have too much noble in us, not to have been consistent once in the good, in which God created us and endowed us with supernatural grace. We have too much capacity of good not to be destined for something much nobler than we at the best are. But "He who made thee without thee, will not save thee without thee." The mass of evil is but the refuse which will not be restored. The simplest self-conquest is the presence of a supernatural power, a fruit of the Passion of Jesus, a triumph of His love and of His hallowing Spirit.

Be not dismayed, then, though men who think that they see, see not, or though they see not, because they think that they see. It is but the condition of the victories of faith over the soul, free, if it will, to be disbelieved. Be not discouraged, if iniquity abound, or mankind seem to deafen itself in its pleasures or gains, or at the stupidity of an intellect which will not acknowledge a God Whom it does not see, or own its own free-will, which it has used against God continually, and, by repeated choices of its own evil against God's good, has well-nigh enslaved to its master-passion, which God would have subjected to it. Jesus foretold at once His victories and His sorrows; His victories in those who willed to look to Him as their Master, their Saviour, their Regenerator, their Life, their Resurrection, their Immortality of Joy; His sorrows, in those who would not be redeemed.

O that we looked, or that we may look, more to Jesus, "the Author and Finisher of our faith!" O that we had

His interests more at our hearts ; that we longed with a burning love, with a fiery zeal, to win more souls to love Him, and to find rest and peace in believing and loving Him! Disappointment there will be, but—

> "E'en disappointment Thou canst bless,
> So love at heart prevail."

Disappointments there will be; but look to Jesus. Ask of Him a heart of fire ; pray Him to touch thy lips with that fiery coal. Thou knowest not what He will do in thee, through thee. Look to Him, simply for Him, that the travail of His soul may be accomplished, and He will work in thee and through thee more than thou darest ask or think. What will it be in that Day to have won one soul to His endless glory and His love!

And now in these poor wanderers[e] who have, we trust, after all their weary, miserable straying, returned to the Good Shepherd, and have been by Him brought back into His fold, remember Him, remember the price of thy own soul, remember thyself.

[e] For a penitentiary.

SERMON VII.

Jonah.

JONAH i. 10.

"Then were the men exceedingly afraid, and said unto him, Why hast thou done this? For the men knew that he fled from the presence of the Lord, because he had told them."

WHEN we take up the Book of Jonah, that which strikes us first of all as lying upon the very surface of the book is the degree in which miracle pervades the whole narrative. In this respect the book is unlike any other among the minor Prophets. Zechariah's earlier prophecies take the form of a series of visions; Jonah's is a history of wonders patent to sense. Jonah thus seems to belong less to the minor Prophets than to the narratives of the Prophets Elijah and Elisha, preserved in the historical books of the Old Testament. His life is a tissue of preternatural occurrences. "Nothing is impossible with God," observes a clever sceptical Commentator, "and hence Jonah lives in the belly of the sea-fish without being suffocated; hence the Palm springs up during the night to such a height that it overshadows a man in a sitting posture. As Jehovah bends everything in the world to His own purposes at pleasure, these marvellous coincidences of his book had nothing in them to astonish the Author. The lot falls upon the right man; the tempest rises most opportunely and is allayed at the proper time; and the fish is ready at hand to swallow Jonah and vomit him out again. So, again, the tree is ready to sprout up, the worm to kill it, and the burning wind to make its loss perceptible*."

Between commentators of this temper and the writer of the Sacred Book the real difference is, that the Scripture writer believes seriously in a living God, and— I must say it, reluctantly but distinctly—the Commentator does not. The Scripture writer certainly takes it for granted that He Who made and Who rules the world, is not precluded from acting on it and in it by any iron laws which fetter His liberty; and that to control creatures and events is not more difficult for Him than to have given them being. Whereas in the mind of the Commentator, the dead abstraction which he calls God is the slave of the living, sensible reality which he names Nature; or rather Nature forms a screen between human life and God, which keeps God very effectively at a distance, and surrounds man with agencies and laws, supposed to do their work like a self-moving clock, and upon whose motion a living Omnipotent Will is never suffered to innovate. For the writers of Holy Scripture miracle is always possible, and the only question is whether there is sufficient evidence for asserting its existence in a particular case. For writers like this Commentator miracle is always impossible, and the only question is, how most easily to get over the authority and statements of Scripture on the subject. Beyond all doubt the Book of Jonah does raise this question as directly as any book in the Bible; perhaps more so.

* Hitzig Einl. qu. by Keil. Einleitung in das Buch. Jon. Biblisch Comm.

Although the preservation of Jonah in the belly of the sea-fish, and the growth of the *Palma Christi* to a sufficient height to overshadow a sitting man, have well-attested analogies in nature which go to make the possibility of such miracles at least conceivable [b] even to the most purely naturalistic imagination; yet the whole narrative is instinct with the presence of a living, all-governing God, Who makes the material world subserve the moral, and Who acts through the lower creatures on the souls of man. In the early ages of Christianity the Book of Jonah was appropriately ridiculed by the heathen Lucian; and in one of his Epistles St. Augustine combats the faintheartedness of some Christian believers who were disposed on this point to wince at hearing of jests current among the pagans. The virtual substance and upshot of St. Augustine's remarks is this, that a man either believes in the Resurrection of Christ or he does not. If he does not; he is not a Christian, at least in any sense known to the New Testament. If he does; he believes in a stupendous miracle which ought to make it logically impossible for him to take exception at other well-attested miracles, such as that of Jonah's sojourn in the belly of the sea-fish [c]. The question is thus in reality a wider and deeper one than any connected with this particular book; and the history of Jonah will be respected and believed by those who are not prepared to make short work with the most solemn and important portions of the Gospel narratives. For our Lord Himself attests the truth of Jonah's history, and makes it a sign or warrant of the miracle which was to prove His own mission to the world: "As Jonah was three days and

[b] Keil Einl., and *in loc.*
[c] Ep. 106, qu. by Dr. Pusey, "Minor Prophets," Introd. to Jonah.

three nights in the whale's belly, even so shall the Son of Man be three days and three nights in the heart of the earth."

Thus much upon a question which could not be entirely passed by, but which we may here brush out of the way of this evening's proper subject. To his own age, doubtless, not less than to ours, Jonah's life was an announcement of the presence and power of the living God in this His own world, which is the work of His Hands, and which most assuredly He has not deserted. But besides this, there are two messages which are spoken to our age and to all from the pages of this book; one of them concerning the love and large-heartedness of God, the other the history of a human soul, which is by no means singular in the moral aspects of its agitated destiny.

I. This will appear if we follow awhile the guidance of the history, and accordingly begin by asking the question, why Jonah was sent to Nineveh?

"Now the word of the Lord came to Jonah the son of Amittai, saying, Arise, go to Nineveh, that great city, and cry against it; for their wickedness is come up before Me [d]."

This commission, it has been observed, was in keeping with God's ordinary providence respecting heathen nations [e]. God always blessed those of the heathen who were brought into contact with His chosen people by a certain knowledge of Himself. The Egyptian kings and people learnt much of Him from Joseph in one generation, and from Moses in another. The Canaanites heard of Him from the Spies; the Philistines by the capture of the Sacred Ark; the Phœnicians on the Mediterranean coast through Hiram of Tyre; the

[d] Jonah i. 1.   [e] Pusey, "Minor Prophets," p. 247.

Syrians of Damascus through captives like Naaman's servant and the miracles of Elisha; the Babylonian and Persian kings through Daniel, and the Persians later through Esther. The truth which was already "the glory of God's people Israel," was, in a measure, "a light to lighten the Gentiles." The Synagogue anticipated some features of the Gospel, as the Church has incorporated and will always retain certain elements of the Law. It is true now that Christians are, in the Apostle's words, "a chosen generation, a royal priesthood, an holy nation, a peculiar people [f]." It was true, then, that "God is no respecter of persons; but in every nation he that feareth Him, and worketh righteousness, is accepted with Him [g]." The laws of the Divine Government are invariable; only in one age prominence is given to one law or principle, in another to another.

Jonah was sent to Nineveh in the meridian of Assyrian greatness. Two monarchs had just died whose reigns had been a succession of victories. Pul, or Ivalush, the first assailant of Israel, was yet to come. Nineveh was great both in its extent and in its power. The circuit of its walls was sixty miles; and although within the large area thus enclosed, as at Babylon, there would have been a considerable acreage of ground under cultivation,—and there is an allusion in this very book to the vast quantities of cattle herded there,—the population of the city was at least 600,000. If, among European capitals, it could not compare as to population with Paris, much less with London; Nineveh must have equalled, if it did not exceed, Berlin or St. Petersburg. Nineveh was a city in which human nature was brutalized by a long career of successful violence; brutalized to a point which degraded it even below the

[f] 1 Pet. ii. 9. [g] Acts x. 34, 35.

average heathen level. The Prophet Nahum finds the natural image which will do justice to its moral characteristics, only in the lions' den: Nineveh, he says, "is the dwelling of the lions, and the feeding-place of the young lions, where the lion did tear in pieces enough for his whelps, and strangled for his lionesses [h]." Nineveh was the home of rapacity, injustice, violence, cruelty, conducted on a truly imperial scale; and God, speaking to Jonah, says, "Their wickedness is come up before Me." God is brought before us in these words, as He sits above this waterflood of crime, as He remaineth in the moral world a King for ever. He is the Great Judge unseen by man, but witnessing all human acts and words and motives, seated even now upon His Throne of Judgment; and each crime of each member of that vast community mounts upwards, and is registered in His Heavenly Court [i]. The same phrase had already been used of the murder of Abel, and of the iniquity of Sodom and Gomorrha; it marks that special notice of sin which precedes a judgment. God had waited long in His Patience and His Mercy, but the cup at length was full to overflowing. The great city of the East must perish; and yet, only forty days before the appointed day of ruin, a voice of warning should reach it, proclaiming the justice yet implying the tenderness of God.

Of that message of mercy Jonah was to be the bearer. Other Prophets might prophesy the future conversion of the heathen to the true God, following upon the surrender of Israel to the heathen power, and upon the appearance and Death of the Messiah; Jonah was to anticipate the Gospel in another way. Jonah's book contains no predictions of the remote future in words;

[h] Nah. ii. 11, 12.   [i] See Pusey *in loc.*

although we know from another source that he did foretell the restoration of the borders of Israel by Jeroboam II.[k] He was, like the Baptist, to be a preacher of repentance, who roused men by warning them of the coming judgments of God. He was to be an Apostle of the Gentiles before the days of Jesus Christ ; a prophet of Israel who was to witness by the great work of his life against the notion that particular peoples and races could have no part in the living God. By going to Nineveh he was to inflict upon the reluctant imagination of his countrymen the truth that " God will have all men to be saved ;" he was to break down the barriers which were supposed to restrain the Divine Mercy within the frontiers of Israel.

His book witnesses to this truth in other ways besides his mission to Nineveh.

What a picture is that of the heathen sailors, of their awe at the presence of a Divine Power in the storm, of their tender and humane consideration for the Hebrew Prophet, of their earnestness in worshipping the idol-deities whom alone they knew, and all this leading up to their final conversion to the true God[l]!

What a moral miracle ; how magnificent in itself ; how great in its significance and bearing on the future of the world is the conversion of Nineveh in the sequel at the Prophet's Voice! For a single day a foreign prophet announces in the streets of Nineveh the coming judgments, and the whole city turns in repentance to God. When we consider the resistance which one human will can offer to the influences of God's grace, and multiply such resistance by the numbers of a vast Asiatic capital, we see that this is really a miracle compared with which the prophet's preservation in the sea-fish

[k] 2 Kings xiv. 25.   [l] Pusey, Jonah.

is altogether insignificant; since the irrational creature would have opposed no resistance whatever to the will of its Creator. It was wrought not among Jews but Gentiles; and our Lord referred to the heathen Ninevites as an example to, and a condemnation of, the men of His day. "The men of Nineveh shall rise up in judgment with this generation, and shall condemn it; because they repented at the preaching of Jonas, and behold a Greater than Jonas is here."

This was, indeed, a foretaste of the Blessed Gospel. To us it seems a simple truth, the capacity of all human beings for salvation, through the knowledge and grace of our God and Saviour. But it was a truth dimly discerned of old; and only brought home in the long run to the conscience of man, by a long tale of sufferings and blood. Are we Christians quite sure that we have really conquered it? Up to the French Revolution, if not since, there was in the French Pyrenees a race of men known as the Cagots. They were said to be descendants of the Arian Goths; but for many centuries they had renounced their error; they believed and worshipped exactly as their neighbours. Yet to this day you may see in the old Pyrenæan churches the small door by which they alone entered and left the aisle assigned to them; the yard where they alone were buried; the lane or street which they alone inhabited; the stream or well of water which supplied them alone, since, to touch it were, in the opinion of their neighbours, downright pollution. Admitted to share the highest spiritual privileges, they were practically treated as a race accursed; they were shunned as the enemies of God and man. The spiritual fellowship which could not be denied them did but make the social ban by which they were oppressed more marked and hateful.

There are no Cagots among us in England. Be it so: but are there no proofs of the same temper as that which proscribed this outcast class? Is not the human heart much the same in England as in France, now as in the last century, and for the matter of that, as it was in Palestine in the days of Jonah? Certainly our Lord has since then stretched out His arms upon the Cross, that He might embrace the world within the compass of His Redemptive Love; but the language which is still to be heard among us about African races, and the practical value of missions, and even about European nations and our Irish fellow-countrymen, and some kindred subjects, shews how little we have understood Him.

II. We pass to the next point; Jonah's conduct, upon receiving the Divine command.

What was Jonah's exact moral position?

Jonah *knew* that God had spoken to him. How the word of the Lord came to him we know not. We only know that it so came to him that he could not doubt whose word it was. There is a phrase used in the Old Testament not unfrequently, "It was said unto" such and such a prophet "*by* the word of the Lord." The rendering should be "*in*, the word of the Lord ᵐ." This phrase seems to represent the 'word of the Lord' as an atmosphere of kindling holy thought, a sphere of spiritual truth encompassing the prophet, illuminating and moving his whole soul, and finally taking shape in language of exhortation, or prediction, or teaching, or resolve, as the case might be. So it may have been with Jonah. We know nothing of events which may have preceded this heavenly inspiration. We know not

בדבר ᵐ

whether his natural tastes, or capacities, or antecedents, whether travel, or friendships, or any like circumstances, led the way. The prophet tells us nothing to satisfy mere curiosity: every word of his book has a moral and spiritual drift. We only know that however it came to him, it was really a message from heaven which came to him, and that he knew it to be so.

This suggests a most interesting and solemn truth. Every human being, be he prophet or layman, has a definite work, some one definite work to do in this world before he dies. It is a work which he alone is fitted by God to do: his stock of strength, of thought, of feeling, of general capacity, his endowments of character, his friendships, his most instinctive and unconscious movements, all have a bearing on it. Others may be in many ways very superior to him; others may be wonderfully like him: but no other human being can fitly take the place assigned to him in the Divine Predestination. "For this cause have I raised thee up," is the motto which points to the crisis, when he will come face to face, in all his liberty, and in all his weakness, with the call to his predestined work. His Nineveh may be, in the eyes of the world, in his own judgment, altogether beyond his powers. It may be, as he imagines, so insignificant as to be quite beneath them. But his responsibility, his danger, his glorious opportunity, are in either case the same, when he stands confronted with the duty which beyond all others was designed for him by the Creator Who gave him life. We only learn the real interest of our own or of other men's lives, when the idea, the possibility of discovering and following out their providential purpose has dawned upon us.

How did Jonah receive the commission which God

gave him? "Jonah rose up to flee unto Tarshish from the presence of the Lord [n]."

What is the state of mind which this implies? Jonah knew God's Will, but he did not welcome it. Why did he not welcome it?

Was it that God commanded exertions from which his constitutional indolence shrank? This has often been taken for granted. But the history discountenances it. They who fly from hard work do not, with their eyes open, undertake exertions which are at least as great as those they would avoid. In those days a voyage along the whole course of the almost unknown Mediterranean was a more serious effort than a journey, familiar enough to an Eastern imagination, by routes which, comparatively, were well frequented across the desert to the great Asiatic capital.

Was it, then, fear? Did Jonah shrink from the violence of those fierce and brutal heathen to whom he was sent? Certainly not. His later history, and, indeed, his conduct on board the ship of Tarshish, shews that he had that perfect confidence in God's protecting Hand which makes fear impossible. He had no real continuing fear even in the belly of the sea-fish: "When my soul fainted within me, I remembered the Lord: and my prayer came in unto Thee into Thine Holy Temple [o]."

What, then, was Jonah's motive for disobedience? He himself tells us that it was a private theory of his own; it was, in fact, a misguided patriotism. When upon their repentance afterwards God pardoned the Ninevites, Jonah, as he tells us, was very angry: "And he prayed unto the Lord, and said, I pray Thee, O

---

[n] Jonah i. 3.   [o] Ibid. ii. 7.

Lord, was not this my saying when I was yet in my country? Therefore I fled before unto Tarshish: for I knew that Thou art a gracious God, and merciful, slow to anger, and of great kindness, and repentest Thee of the evil [p]." Jonah had no doubt of God's mercy; he feared lest God's mercy should be shewn to those whom he knew to be the enemies of his country. He knew that Assyria would be the scourge of Israel, and he therefore wished that the sins of Assyria might draw down upon it a speedy vengeance such as should disable it for purposes of aggression. If he obeyed the command of God, and denounced against Nineveh the coming judgments; God, he knew, was so tender towards all signs of repentance, especially in those who had had scanty opportunities, that He probably would not fulfil the judgments after all. Let Nineveh, then, be left to itself, to its vast ever-increasing body of sin, to its sure inheritance of coming wrath; and let Israel—the people of the Lord, the country of the Prophet—be spared from anxiety and peril in the years to come.

Patriotism, my brethren, is a natural instinct, which Revelation has, at least indirectly, sanctioned. As our family, so our country is God's gift; and the instinctive love of country, like that of near relatives, which every good man should feel, is His gift also. But neither the love of family or country is God's best gift to man; and it may happen that a stronger and holier passion than either, namely, the love of God Himself, will, under certain circumstances, demand a serious sacrifice on the part of these lower affections. We ought, indeed, before we sacrifice them, to be very sure that some subtle form of selfishness is not playing us a trick; and

[p] Jonah iv 2.

that it *is* the love of God, and not of something much lower than He, and perhaps very unlike Him, which exacts the offering. But Abraham had had such an assurance, and it was his glory to have obeyed it, tender parent as he was[q]; Jonah had such an assurance, but in Jonah the Jewish patriot, watching anxiously for the signs of the political horizon, was stronger than the Prophet and guide of men listening only for the commands of the Most High. No doubt, in Jonah's case, the natural sentiment of patriotism was reinforced by the religious feeling of the Israelite in favour of the privileges of the Covenant people: as a theocrat not less than as a patriot, Jonah would leave Nineveh to its fate. But this was, in Jonah, a sin against the light. Prophet as he was, he knew God's Mind; opened partly in earlier ages; opening yet more distinctly in his own; opened at last with indisputable clearness to his own soul,—respecting the Gentile races. He knew that they were to have a share in the Heart of God.

The peasantry around his village home on the hills of Zabulon might naturally and rightly feel as he did. But then Jonah was not a simple peasant, but a Prophet to boot; and he could not, if he would, act with only a peasant's light and a peasant's responsibilities. It was not for him to reflect popular prejudice when he ought to be guiding it; and he might have known from the history of his country that in the end the best patriot is not the man who lends himself to the political passion of the age or of the hour, but he who, at whatever cost and beyond all else, serves his God.

Can we Christians say that, with the love of the Incarnation around us, we have always remembered that in the Body of Christ there is neither Greek nor

[q] Gen. xxii. 16, 17.

Jew, circumcision nor uncircumcision, barbarian nor Scythian, bond or free, since all are one in Christ Jesus'? Has this conviction availed to stop the bloody wars which have desolated Christendom, and the real reasons for which have continually been of the most earthly kind? Have we constantly acted on that precept of our Divine Master which bids His followers, in person or by deputy, go into all the world and preach the Gospel to every creature*? Enough has been said of those ancient British Bishops who are reported to have been unwilling to convert the Saxon enemies of their race to the Faith of Christ, lest conversion should save them from a punishment which their barbarities deserved. But what shall we say of the policy both of France and England in Eastern Europe at this very moment, which from jealousy of another Christian power condemns twelve millions of Christians to enslavement beneath the yoke of the Infidel? What of the principle of our old Indian rule, which for so many years discouraged Christian missions in the interests of commerce; or of a war with China, undertaken with the object of forcing upon that country a demoralising traffic which even its heathen conscience condemned? If Christians can thus forget themselves and their Lord, let us not marvel at the Israelite Prophet, who had solid reasons for his error, the very shadow of which has been taken from us.

Jonah rose up. He could not sit still. He could not go on quietly in his village home as if nothing had happened to him; as if he was morally in exactly the same state as that in which he had been before the word of the Lord bade him go to Nineveh. If he

---

' Col. iii. 11; 1 Cor. xii. 13; Rom. x. 12; Gal. iii. 28, v. 6; Eph. vi. 8. * St. Mark xvi. 15.

did not obey God, he must do something else; he must get out of God's way, or if that were impossible, he must try to forget Him. Jonah rose up to flee unto Tarshish from the presence of the Lord.

Here let us guard against a grave misunderstanding. Jonah did not suppose that he could literally escape from the presence of God. He did not suppose that there were corners in the universe, still less in the inhabited globe, from which the Presence and Power of its Maker is excluded. Such a conception was natural, it may be, to the heathen, with their many gods, presiding, like human governors, or patrons, over territorial districts assigned to them by the imaginations of men,—districts beyond the limits of which they had no real jurisdiction, and could therefore be set at defiance with more or less prospect of impunity. But Jonah knew that God is everywhere by the necessity of His Nature. A localized Deity would be no god at all to a soul which had once looked the Incomprehensible in the face. The devotional language of Israel was ever the same: "Whither shall I go then from Thy Spirit? or whither shall I go from Thy Presence? If I climb up into heaven Thou art there, if I go down to hell Thou art there also: If I take the wings of the morning, and remain in the uttermost parts of the sea, even there shall Thy Hand lead me, and Thy right Hand shall hold me[t]." And Jonah's prayer, embodying as it does so much of the Psalter, alone shews that he was not ignorant of a truth, which was indeed as elementary in the creed of a Jewish believer as it is in that of a Christian.

The words "from the presence of the Lord" should be rendered "from being before the Lord." It was

[t] Ps. cxxxix. 7—10.

not God's inevitable and encompassing Presence, but his own sense of standing before Him as His servant and minister, from which Jonah fled. Distinguish between God's actual, matter-of-fact, unseen, but all-encompassing presence, and our personal sense of it. From the first escape is impossible; from the last it is, alas! only too easy. What Jonah wanted was a distraction, which should relieve him from the sense of duty which belonged to his prophet-conscience, from those scruples which the mistaken patriot within him would fain have crushed. He would change the mental and spiritual atmosphere; he would turn his back on a country where all that met the eye spoke of the power and reality of the Sinaitic Revelation; he would interest himself in human life, under other and different aspects; the language, the commerce, the customs, if not the religion of the Spanish sea-port, might give a turn to his thoughts which would enable him to forget the past. So he "went down to Joppa, and found a ship going to Tarshish; and he paid the fare thereof and went down into it, to go with them unto Tarshish from being before the Lord ⁿ."

My brethren, Tarshish and the Phœnician trading-vessel belong to a civilization which has long been buried out of sight. But the human soul remains at this hour true to its old instincts and to its oft-repeated history. We still hear the Divine summons to hard or unwelcome duty; and there are modern methods of flight unto Tarshish from being before the Lord, which do at least as well as the Phœnician trader. A change of friends, a change of habits, a change of literary occupations may suffice. Tarshish is near

ⁿ Jonah i. 3.

enough to all of us to make it easy for us to forget our duties to Nineveh.

III. Enough has been already said on the preternatural aspects of the judgment which overtook Jonah. Morally speaking, it brings before us three great truths. First, God's mercy in not leaving Jonah to himself. The storm was sent in love rather than in justice. If Jonah had been a reprobate, he would probably have reached Tarshish in perfect safety, after a very favourable voyage. Whom the Lord loveth He chasteneth. When we have done a deliberately wrong act, entangling and blinding the conscience, and giving to the whole moral being a false direction, the best thing that can happen to us is a heavy judgment, — some mighty tempest in the sea of life,—which rouses conscience into activity, and makes any effort or sacrifice welcome, if only thereby the past may be retraced.

Secondly, Jonah acquiesces in, nay, he dictates the terms of his own punishment. He was not dragged over the ship's sides against his will. The storm had spoken not to his physical fear, but to his conscience; his conscience was lashed into an agony which rendered him indifferent to the surging fury of the waves. He had to pass through a humiliating yet most healthful punishment, which they only can suffer who stand in some position of superiority towards their fellow-men. When little children remark misconduct or inconsistency in their parents, or servants in their master, or laymen in their clergyman; the words which express in the speaker a genuine embarrassment are felt by the hearer to convey, however unconsciously, the severest censure. "Then were the men exceedingly afraid, and said unto him, Why hast thou done this[x]?" The sincere

[x] Jonah i. 10.

wonder of the poor heathen inflicts upon the prophet of the Divine will a rebuke which they do not even suspect. Jonah had just told them, "I am an Hebrew: and I fear the Lord the God of heaven, Which hath made the sea and the dry land[^]." Their words express the distressed amazement which was produced by comparing the Prophet's profession of faith with his actual practice. If he really believed in such a God as this, how could he dare to disobey Him? It is the inconsistency of believers which is the wonder of those who believe not, and the worst enemy of the Faith. It is the patent and inexplicable inconsistency of professing to believe in the Eternal Son of God, Incarnate and Crucified for the sins of men, and then of living, as our consciences tell us many of us do live, in utter practical forgetfulness of this Powerful and Loving Saviour. Much is said, and truly, in these days, of the increased boldness and earnestness of infidelity in attacking the fundamental truths of Christianity: and there never was a time when Scepticism had at its command so much ability, so many literary organs, so large and imposing an array of distinguished names, in England, as the present. But of this let us Christians be sure ;—that when unbelief has said its last and bitterest word against the Person and Authority of our Divine Lord, it has done much less towards deposing Him from His rightful Throne in the hearts of men, than we individually can do, may I not add, have done, by our practical disloyalty to our own convictions, by the broken, halting, inconsistent service which, at the best, we render Him. Jonah felt something like this as to his narrower creed ; and when the heathen sailors asked him for guidance, he uttered the sentence of his own punishment: "Take

Jonah i. 9.

me up and cast me forth into the sea: so shall the sea be calm unto you; for I know that for my sake this tempest is come upon you ᶻ."

Thirdly, Jonah's punishment brought with it an opportunity, which most of God's judgments in this world do offer us, and of which he made the most. The belly of the sea-fish was a retreat, from which the world was excluded. In it Jonah was driven back upon himself and the One Being, Who is like self, in being never really absent from any among us. Instead of occupying himself with plans for escape, or abandoning himself to despair, Jonah returned to God, from Whose presence he had fled, in earnest communion. He did not invent new prayers; but he fell back upon Psalms which already enriched the devotions of Israel, and with which he had long been familiar. They said all that he wanted and more; just as a few inspired words have before now fed the soul of a dying Christian for weeks or months without being exhausted. And thus Jonah was emptied for the time of his waywardness, and was at length restored to a liberty which he at once devoted to God's Will. "Then the Lord spake unto the fish, and it vomited out Jonah. So Jonah arose and went to Nineveh ᵃ."

IV. The lessons of a history like Jonah's may easily be misapplied. Many cases may occur in modern life which seem to be parallel, but are not so in reality. There is one feature of Jonah's case which ought to be kept steadily in view, in order to prevent such misapplications; and that is, the fact that he was himself personally convinced, and upon sufficient grounds, that God had spoken to him, and desired him to go to Nineveh.

ᶻ Jonah i. 12. ᵃ Ibid. ii. 10; iii. 3.

This fact seems to be lost sight of in a class of cases, to which Scriptural examples, like Jonah, are not unfrequently applied, as sanctions. I mean cases in which, without the opportunity or the disposition to examine the questions really at issue, persons are tempted to join the Roman Catholic Church. There have been of course many instances, of which we all have heard or known, in which after thought and prayer, and study, persons have come to the conclusion that it is their duty to become Roman Catholics. Now, while as English Churchmen we cannot but think them wrong, either as to their facts, or at least as to the inferences they draw from such facts, or in both respects; it is not to such cases as these that what I am going to say applies. In a larger number of cases men and women who are disposed to become Roman Catholics, do not really study any one of the questions at issue; and the force which impels them towards Rome is rather an unthinking impulse than a conviction. This impulse is probably made up of several ingredients; partly of a natural taste for art or organization; partly of the love of change as such, which enters so largely into all our natures; partly of a notion that in the Roman Church it would be possible to make a new spiritual start, and do better than had been done in the Church of England; partly of a strong affection for some friend who has taken the step in past years, and who is anxious to enlist recruits for his new communion. Under the pressure of this strong composite impulse a man meets with a Roman Catholic; who, as a matter of course, tells him that this impulse is itself a Divine Grace, drawing him sensibly towards the kingdom of the Truth, and that to resist it is perilous. "You are Jonah," the Roman Catholic says to him in effect, "and you are bound to make a sacrifice "and to obey the truth, at the cost of going to Nineveh. "If you take your own course, if you resist this impulse "which is upon you, you are really taking the road to "Tarshish; and, if you are not to be lost altogether, the "best thing that can happen to you is some terrible "judgment which will bring you to your senses."

In minds of a certain order, this kind of inaccurate appeal to Scripture supersedes the necessity of further argument. They are keenly—not too keenly—alive to the reality of God's guiding and sustaining grace; they are fearful—not too fearful—of grieving His Holy Spirit; but they are not sufficiently accurate to observe the fallacy which underlies such a use of Holy Scripture. That fallacy consists in the assumption that the path of duty is really as clear to themselves as it was to the Hebrew Prophet. Jonah had no doubt about—no reason for doubting—God's Will that he should go to Nineveh; there was no real room for argument in the matter; he resisted what he knew to be a direct Divine command on the strength of a private, and chiefly political view or prejudice. But in the case before us, the question whether God does command a man to join the Church of Rome is the very point at issue. The mere existence of a strong impulse in the direction of Rome does not decide this point any more than the existence of a strong impulse in a very opposite direction proves the truth of Calvinism, or of Socinianism. Before the impulse can be treated as a grace, or as anything but a disturbing and misleading force, which ought to be expelled and excluded from the soul as quickly as may be, the rectitude of the course of action towards which the impulse leads should be satisfactorily established. In Jonah's case this was done; but in the case before us, it has not yet been done. No English Churchman can satisfy himself that it is a duty to become a Roman Catholic, until he has at least satisfied himself of two points. First, he must be sure that the Church of England *is not*—I do not say, a perfect representative in all respects of the Primitive Church of Christ, (few men of adequate information and honesty would assert that she is)—but that she is not—a portion of Christ's Body at all; that she is a dead branch of a Divine Tree, or a mere piece of State-contrivance. Secondly, he must satisfy himself that the Roman Catholic Church *is*,—I do not say, a part of the Church of Christ, with errors and shortcomings, and also with blessings all her own, (she is that beyond all doubt),—but that she *alone* is—the Holy Body; that she *alone* on earth represents, and that she represents adequately, to this generation, the fair form and pure countenance and unsullied soul of the Church of the Apostles. If a man says that he has been able to overcome what appear to be the absolutely insuperable difficulties which lie against deciding these points in the Roman sense ; we can only feel surprise and regret ; but it is quite in order that he should proceed to strengthen his motives to action by the instance of Jonah. But until he has done this ; until he has thus satisfied himself, as far as he can, that God's will really does point in the same direction as his personal impulse ; to appeal to Jonah, or to other examples of obeying or disobeying real calls of God in Scripture, is to beg the whole question which ought to be at issue ; it is to do, however unconsciously, a violence to the true teaching of Scripture, and to play a trick of a very serious kind with the conscience itself.

And if Jonah's case has no bearings upon those

who are hesitating, on adequate grounds, as to the path of duty; still less does it say anything to those who are conscientiously satisfied that God has not called them to the duty which Jonah's example is employed to recommend.

A man is invited to accept some work for which he believes himself to be unfitted. It is a great and noble work; it is pressed upon him by persons who have high claims to respect and deference at his hands; it addresses itself not merely to his imagination, to his ambition, to his spirit of enterprise, but to higher things in him than these, to his love of God and of his fellow-men, to his desire to do good in his generation. But he knows himself not to be the right man for it. It is not merely that he has a general sense of unworthiness to undertake that or anything else, such as is professed, conventionally by everybody, and sincerely by good men, on all similar occasions: but he is conscious of particular deficiencies, and of particular positive features of his character, which make it certain that he must fail, if he attempts that specific work. This being so, whatever authority may say to him, he would fall below the commercial level of morality if he were to undertake the work in question; since such an undertaking implies an engagement on his part to produce certain results, which he knows himself to be distinctly unable to produce, in consequence of those defects or tendencies upon which he can lay his finger, and which incapacitate him for doing so. It is easy to say that we ought to trust to the grace of God to make up the deficiency: but, in ordinary cases of this sort, grace perfects natural tendencies, it does not create powers which do not exist in a natural germinal form. His friends may say, You are Jonah, and that is your

Nineveh. But if Jonah had been unable to walk or to use his voice, either a miracle would have been wrought, or he would not have been sent on his errand. In all such cases the real question to be answered before all others is, whether the man has been called to this work by God at all? Of every such call there are two component parts, the outward voice and pressure of authority or circumstance, and the inward response and ratification of the conscience. Where this last is not found, there God has not as yet really spoken; and it is not found, if men are honest with themselves, when they are conscious of specific incapacity to discharge duties which circumstances appear to thrust upon them.

But if this history may be easily misapplied, it is much more likely in our day to be neglected altogether. It is almost impossible to exaggerate the moral value of such a history, whether for the purposes of warning or of encouragement.

Wherever the path of duty is clear, and it is deserted for some reason that seems to have a great deal in it, but that will not meet the eye of God—or for no real reason at all,—there the moral features of Jonah's history, under different outward circumstances, repeat themselves.

Take the case of a clergyman who has reached middle life, and whose conscience distinctly tells him that he ought to do more for God's glory than he has done yet. He sees now for the first time what his office really implies, but he is attracted by some private and secular opinion or taste, which turns him aside from obedience to God's voice within him. After all, he says to himself, there are other ways of doing good; it is possible to do good with less of professional narrowness, and more of a broad human spirit than in the clerical life.

Possibly, as with Jonah, the patriot within him becomes the foe of the prophet: he will serve his country in this world, and let others help his countrymen, if they can, towards the next. He resolves, as the phrase is, to "give up being a clergyman." Of course he cannot really forego his responsibilities, or erase from his soul the indelible stamp of his consecration to God's service, any more than he can scratch out the ineffaceable marks of his baptismal privileges. Before God and His angels, throughout eternity as in time, for weal or in woe, he is an ordained man; the gifts and calling of God being in this as in other ways, without recall, and repentance. But doubtless as far as the world goes, he can, if he so desires, forego all that proclaims his spiritual character; he can dress like a layman, talk like a layman, betake himself, so far as the law will allow, to lay occupations, and distinguish himself even among laymen by his ostentatiously anti-clerical tastes. In other words he can "fly to Tarshish" from being before the Lord as His servant and minister. Happy, indeed, if he is not permitted to reach his goal; happy, if, overtaken by a tempest of adverse circumstances, he is thrown in his agony into a retirement which buries him for awhile away from the face of man, and enables him to commune with his God, and to understand his inalienable responsibilities, in full view of the realities of life and death. Better, doubtless, it were never to have fled to Tarshish; but if the error have been made, the storm and the whale's belly are but pledges of a Love Which will not leave him to himself.

Or take the somewhat analogous case of a younger man who has formed a serious intention of serving God in Holy Orders, and in such a mind, comes up to this University. He has had no other plan for life; the desire has been strongest in him in his best and holiest moments; his natural dispositions, the wishes of his parents, and above all his sense of the solemnity of life, and of the majesty and necessity of revealed Truth, have moulded his purpose. When he has heard of the poverty and crime which are distancing the best efforts of modern society to overtake them, and others have talked of social science congresses, of economical statistics, of new efforts at legislation; a voice within him has said clearly, distinctly, Arise, go unto Nineveh. When, turning the eye of his soul within, he has observed the various evidences of an indestructible life-principle, and has reflected upon the priceless value of one undying soul—his own,—or on the responsibilities of each towards all, and of all towards each; the word has come to him, saying, Arise, go unto Nineveh. And when, looking out of and away from himself, he has beheld Jesus Christ our Lord dying upon the Cross of Shame, dying for him as for all, "that they which live should not henceforth live unto themselves, but unto Him That died for them, and rose again;" the word of the Lord has been again heard within his soul, Arise, go unto Nineveh. If he can trust any instinct for good, if he can trust any clear intimation of destiny, if he can surrender himself to any certain verdict of conscience, he is bound to devote himself to the spiritual work of the Church of Christ.

He comes to Oxford, hoping to find nothing but sympathy, encouragement, guidance, for all the noblest and highest aspirations within him. But a voice here whispers to him too often,—in a less religious spirit than Jonah's political theories,—and certainly not in the spirit of the Word of God to Jonah: "Is it not "better to live for this world of which we are sure, than

"for the next world, which at best is a matter of specu-
"lation? Is it not a greater distinction to wear the
"livery of an earthly service, than that of a clerical
"caste? Are not the clergy—the country clergy—
"wanting in breadth and culture? Do they not pass
"their lives between district visitors, and coal-tickets,
"and blanket-societies, and soup-distributions, and the
"visits of school-inspectors and missionary deputations,
"and church decorations, and the infinite pettinesses
"and details of village or country-town life? Is it not
"better to sit loosely to theological systems, or rather
"to sit above them; to do good in a general unprofes-
"sional way; to be less clerical and more human; to
"take a practical view of life, which shall leave theology
"with all its encumbrances of sentiment and passion to
"minds of a lower and narrower make?" Why, after all, should he go to Nineveh; why not go down at once to Joppa, and pay his fare, and embark for Tarshish?

And so ten or fifteen or twenty years pass by; he is in the midst of the sea of life, with all its interest, but with all its liabilities. "They that go down to that sea in ships, and occupy their business in great waters, these men see the works of the Lord and His wonders in the deep. For at His Word the stormy wind ariseth which lifteth up the waves thereof: they go up to the heaven and down again to the deep; their soul melteth away because of the trouble[b]." Happy and blessed, indeed, are such when it is so; when a great reverse of fortune, or a bitter heartache, or an illness which makes death and judgment realities, forces them into retreat from the mistakes to which they have surrendered them-selves, and to real converse with God. It may be too late then really to attempt what might have been easy

[b] Ps. cvii. 23 -26.

in early years; it may be impossible, when the shadows are lengthening year by year upon the plain, to set out for Nineveh. Yet failure in trying to do right is better than inaction; and an intention to serve God than a wish, more or less disguised, to forget Him.

But Jonah need not be a clergyman; and Nineveh may represent other than clerical fields of work. Jonah may be an eldest son, whom God has blessed with a large property, perhaps in Ireland, and to whose soul He has whispered, that this property, which enables him to be of use to hundreds, perhaps to thousands of poor people, has grave responsibilities. The possession of this property enables him to do that which no steward, no relation, can do for him; this property, and his work in it and for it, is his Nineveh. He has, he can have, no doubt about the outward or the inward elements of his call. God speaks to him both through circumstances, and in the sanctuary of conscience, with equal clearness.

Now suppose him to try to persuade himself that some other line of life, which may have undoubted claims upon others, but which involves his leaving the care of his property to relatives or officials, is the best for him; what is this but a fleeing to Tarshish from being before the Lord? For, layman as he is, this young man is also a prophet; he occupies a position which enables him to insist upon many great moral and spiritual truths before a large circle of people, who will receive them with the same attention and interest from the lips of no other human being. If he foregoes this duty, through an error of self-will; if he leaves the truth unsaid and the good undone, which he, of all men, might best, if not alone, say and do; he is treading most certainly in the footsteps of Jonah. It may be that life will flow on smoothly and prosperously with him, and that he will grow old without finding out the truth; but it will be better for him if it be otherwise. It will be better for him far, if some great failure or misfortune leads him to review his responsibilities as God's Providence defines them, and if, while he yet has life and health to do so, he arises and goes to his Nineveh, at the word of the Lord.

Jonah's history is full of solemn warning: but it is also full of encouragement. It sheds light upon the meaning of a great deal of the suffering which meets us in life. Of the pain which we witness around us, some is purely penal, some belongs to our moral education, some to mysteries of the Divine government which we shall never fathom in this life. But a large department of human pain comes under the same category as the chastisement of Jonah. By a reverse of fortune, or the death of a near relative, or a severe illness, God stops men on their voyage towards some self-chosen Tarshish: He plunges them beneath the waves of adversity while yet He provides an asylum in which their moral life is preserved, in which they may turn to Him in penitence and sincerity. Oh! blessed mystery of His Providence, often witnessed, but little understood, when the barrier of self-will, in all its forms, is gradually but firmly broken down in the soul, and at length there is one prayer stronger and more frequent than any other—a Christian paraphrase of the prayer of Jonah :—

> "Wash me and dry these bitter tears,
> O let my heart no further roam,
> 'Tis Thine, by vows, and hopes, and fears,
> Long since—O call Thy wanderer home ;
> To that dear home, safe in Thy wounded Side,
> Where only broken hearts their shame and sin may hide."

But to understand these great truths, the solemnity of life, the tremendous power which we each and all possess of throwing it away, the reality of God's guidance in it, if we will look out for tokens of His will within and without us, and the blessedness of all suffering which brings us after wilful error to our senses, we must do that which is difficult at the outset of life, we must place ourselves, in thought, at its close.

It is when the clouds are gathering, hour by hour more and more thickly over the sky of time, when the pulse of strength is sensibly ebbing, and the distant horizons of eternity are coming more and more distinctly each moment into view, that the real importance of the lessons of Jonah's history become apparent. It is in those hours, hours they must be of dread perplexity, if they are not hours of resigned hope, that a voice like that of the Tyrian seamen whispers to conscience over some great mistake, then seen first by the soul in its true proportions, Why hast thou done this? It is too late to prescribe self-humiliation and self-punishment, when the margin of life leaves no room for sacrifices, such as might retrieve the unfaithfulness of the past. God may indeed see and accept a pure intention; but it is surely better not to risk an anxiety of which the event may well be doubtful. God grant that we may pray Him sincerely to shew us each "the way that we should walk, since we lift up our souls unto Him;" and that when His promise, "I will inform thee and teach thee in the way wherein thou shalt go, and I will guide thee with Mine eye," is made good to us, we may indeed discern His guidance and obey it.

SERMON VIII.
Elijah.

---

1 KINGS xviii. 21.

"If the Lord be God, follow Him: but if Baal, then follow him."

ELIJAH is distinguished from the rest of the prophets by very marked peculiarities. His Arab-like demeanour and garb, his startling appearances and as rapid flights, his stern grandeur and wild movements, are, at least as a whole, unlike any other of the race of the prophets. Still more deeply does the distinction reach. The majestic character of his miracles was enough to mark him off as singularly gifted. His commanding the three years' famine at his word, the prolonging it another half year because Ahab repented not, the fire descending at his call as he offered the sacrifice on Carmel, the sudden destruction of the captains and their fifties, till the last captain and his company knelt at his feet acknowledging his irresistible power, his going forth to die with apparently the knowledge that the chariot of fire and the horses of fire waited for him in the wilderness,—these and other like signs of power stand out prominently among the miraculous records of the Old Testament. Even in his despondency and timid flight there was an unspeakable greatness about Elijah. The angel minister, the journey of "forty days and forty nights" "in the strength of that meat;" the solitude in the cave of Horeb, God passing by him, revealing the order of the dispensations in the "strong wind," "the earthquake," "the fire," the "still small voice," as he stood at the entering in of the cave, wrapped in the mysterious mantle,—are all circumstances instinct with supernatural dignity.

Then, again, his whole history, from the first sojourning at the brook Cherith to the flight to Horeb, is intensified in its depth of interest because of his remarkable loneliness. Whether in the widow's house at Sarepta, or in the crowd of the worshippers of Baal on Mount Carmel in the face of the king, he was as entirely alone as when he lay under the juniper tree, and wished to die. The chief events of his life were over when Elisha joined him. Nor was it a mere external loneliness. It was a constant peculiar inward heart-consciousness of loneliness and utter lack of sympathy, that he experienced, as he bore his witness for God. He had no idea, until God revealed it to him, of any of the thousands in Israel, that had not "bowed the knee to the image of Baal." He had habitually felt the oppressiveness of what he so bitterly complained before God; "And I only am left, and they seek my life to take it away[a]."

Moreover, all this wonderful range of extraordinary power is enhanced by the exceeding mystery in which he first appears, and in which he departs from the world. Like Melchizedek, he cannot be traced in his parentage or in his home. Like another Enoch, he returns to God without passing through death; while, unlike Enoch, he leaves a deep impression on the mind of his people, that he may at any hour appear again.

But we are chiefly concerned this evening with the

[a] 1 Kings xix. 10.

enquiry as to Elijah's message to the age and people among whom he appeared.

One circumstance strikes us as almost peculiar to him. His message was limited to his age; he was not a seer of the future; no prophecies, properly so called, have come to us through him. The three prophetic utterances which he carried out were limited to his own lifetime; they were fulfilled in Elisha, in Hazael, and in Jehu. He revealed no new truths; he did not expand the vision of the Faithful of his age; he did not advance the evangelical development of the Mosaic system, like Isaiah. He seemed in truth to have in him little of the Teacher. No one sought him for instruction as they did Samuel; nor did he expand the compass of instruction of his age, like Elisha, who sat in the schools of the prophets. He came and went as a meteor. He kept aloof from his kind, descending at his will into the midst of the people under special impulses, as suddenly to retire, withdrawn into his impenetrable solitude again.

Yet no prophet could have left a deeper impression on his age than did Elijah. What more specially strikes us in him is the remarkable unity of his aim. The absorbed character of his life is the point that gives to it its peculiar intensity and grandeur of effect. It is said by philosophers, that for a man to produce the greatest influence, he must pursue and carry out one overmastering idea. Elijah was specially a man of a single purpose. Probably the explanation of his remarkable depression, when he fled from the face of Jezreel into the wilderness, is to be found in this characteristic feature of his mind. It is the habit of a mind possessed with one all-prevailing idea, to become more than ordinarily desponding at failure. There is no relief arising from other mental interests which a variety of objects promotes.

With regard to Elijah's message, his name assists us. It is well known that in the earliest ages, when words really represented things, names also were expressive of the characters of persons. And Elijah's name is manifestly significant. Its meaning is, "The Lord He is God;" "Jehovah is God." The name most accurately describes his message to his people. He came forth at a period in the history of his race when God had been almost renounced. Ahab was king, and he had set himself to establish in the sanctuaries of Israel the idolatry of Phœnicia. Jezebel, the daughter of a priest of Baal, sat with him on the throne. The early calf-worship of Egypt, to which the people were always prone, had developed into complete Baalism. Jericho had just been rebuilt in defiance of the solemn curse pronounced by Joshua. The priests of Baal that ministered at Carmel numbered 750, and they were the sole acknowledged representatives of the priesthood of Israel. Baalism had in fact become the established religion of the country; the priests of the Lord were proscribed, a few only lingering in the land, supported in secret by such as Obadiah. At this crisis Elijah suddenly appears, and his one message, to enforce which his life was devoted, was the assertion of the to us simple truth of the Unity of the true God, and His sole absolute claim on His creatures. Elijah was the link between Moses and our blessed Lord in the assertion of this primal truth. Other prophets we may value more, because they tell us more of Christ; they more directly foreshadow the Gospel. We are wont to assume the unity and supremacy of the Godhead as unquestioned truths; they are presupposed in the

Gospel. But if you put yourself back to the time of Ahab, and remember how at that time the line of Mosaic teaching had almost run out in Israel, that David's throne was occupied by the worshippers of Baal, and no voice was heard throughout the land against the revolution of religious ideas that had taken place, and the altar of the Lord, thrown down, had made way for the worship and ritual of Tyre and Sidon,—you may imagine what to his own age Elijah was, and what an important position he occupies in the chain of witnesses to the truth.

But it was not merely to this truth itself, nakedly considered, that Elijah's momentous testimony relates. There is a cold and barren witness which leaves the truth much as it finds it; it may be no more than an abstract, unpractical, unattractive idea, winning no hearts, subduing no consciences, stirring no convictions, making no partizans, working no change in the popular and current opinions of the day; a witness having no warmth in itself, and generating no warmth in others. Such is the tone in which the ancient philosophers discussed truth. They often thought out great and true ideas of God, and of man's relation to God. But they never formed a life; they had no creative power; they never moved hearts; they presented to the mind simply intellectual ideas coolly and calmly reasoned out Their revelations were like statues, often beautiful statues, and they grew on the pages of what seemed all but inspired writers; but they remained there exercising no influence on the world, and waiting for the fire to descend from heaven to enkindle the forms o beauty, and make them breathe.

Now the revelation, or rather the re-assertion of the truth of the simple and absolute Godhead of Jehovah by Elijah, was a revival wholly distinct from such philosophies. And the singular power of his message lay in this, that what he taught, he taught with a fervour which carried along with it a revolution of the mind of the nation. I have already alluded to Elijah's wildness of demeanour, his rapidity of movement, his ntensity of speech and action. These were but outward signs of the inner man. They were signs of the fiery energy with which the truth that he revered was held. The warmth that lacked in the grandest forms of classical Paganism, glowed richly within Elijah, and it was the combination of the two powers in such singular force that formed the characteristic influence of this great prophet. He bore not merely, like Jonah, a message of repentance to his people; nor was he merely, like Jeremiah, one who mourned deeply the sins of his race; nor, like Elisha, merely a marvellous manifestation of superhuman miraculous power. Elijah stands out above all others in this,—that he grounded his call to repentance on the most vivid and exciting revival of the great Mosaic revelation of Almighty God, and His single and supreme claim on the adoration of mankind. Through the almost fierce aspect of his strong appeal, his mastery of majestic sternness, he seemed in his own person to reproduce the thunders of Sinai, the trumpet-call of the great commandments of the Law. It was in him the union of a revelation, not really new indeed, but new practically, from the utter decline into which it had fallen,—the union of a grand revelation with the intensest inward fire, which formed the force that bore Elijah on, alone, confronting an infidel people, and a sovereign degraded and deeply superstitious; enabling him to raise from the dust the fabric of the ruined faith, the wreck of the altar of

God which had fallen down. To judge Elijah aright, we must combine these two ideas ; not the mere assertion of the supremacy of the true God, nor merely his dauntless energy of fiery zeal, but the two united in the one person, the perfect coalescing of a soul-enthralling truth and an over-mastering mental inspiration.

No wonder that Elijah, long after he had passed away, still spoke to his people. No wonder that he ever lived in the traditions of his race. No wonder that he seemed to them to be the reviver of all new revelations in their after religious history. No wonder that his name became as a household word, intimately associated with all fresh manifestations of God ; that he was ever looked for to return as the herald of every mighty change in the series of the dispensations, the deathless Voice echoing through the advancing ages, the messenger of the New Covenant, the forerunner of Christ in His first Advent, and equally the harbinger of His last tremendous visitation in His second Coming ; that he was ever known, dreaded or desired according to the spiritual condition of the people, as " the Elias that was to come."

And this leads us on to the second branch of the subject assigned to me. For we have to learn from what has been said the message which Elijah bears through all time, and trace its special application to our own age. If we were to fix on any one defective and alarming characteristic of our age in respect of its religious life, as compared perhaps with any past period of our history, it would I think be this,—an unsettlement as to all foundations of faith, even as to the very nature of faith ; a throwing open of first principles, as things to be fought out, or rather as no longer prin-

K 2

ciples but opinions; an upsetting of all time-honoured traditions, and a readiness to accept any new view or theory of belief from any quarter, and enshrine it by the side, if not in the place, of the ancient faith of the One Living and life-giving God, as the Catholic Apostolic Church has ever taught concerning Him. The substance, the stamina of the ancient faith has to be re-constituted; the very primary articles of the Creed have to be maintained in their original truth. And this is needed to be done in all simplicity, by appealing to the fountain head, by going direct to the primary principles of revelation, in order to re-establish the soul of a people, shaken and distracted by years of controversy, aggravated beyond measure by the collision of partizans of a keenly intellectual and daringly speculative age. This was specially in his day Elijah's work, only under very different conditions. His mission was not to build up anything new; it was to repair "the altar of the Lord that was broken down." It was restoration, not reform, nor development; the re-creating a true antiquity, not an accommodation to modern thought. And his refuge in difficulty, when he would recruit his strength and rekindle his failing fires, was to the original home of the faith,—not even to the Evangelical Church of the future,—it was to Horeb, the old well-known Mount of the Law. He would rather re-knit the broken chain of faith to the past, than to the certainly developing future.

And he used no argument. He seemed to disdain reasoning; he made no effort to convince; he but urged a simple direct appeal to the dormant conscience. His teaching turned upon a self-evident alternative; "How long halt ye between two opinions? If the Lord be God, follow Him; but if Baal, then follow him." His powerful appeal to the old faith of Israel against the Babel cry of Baalim seems to be significant of the conflicts of our own time; for he arose to assert the truth when "midday was past," and "the time of the offering of the evening sacrifice was come." So we are contending for the truth when the world has passed its zenith, and the end is felt as though it were rapidly approaching amid the lengthening shadows of the latter days.

We cannot hope to change the character of an age, but we may discern the true spirit to regulate our own life. We need not presume to teach others, when we are humbly learning how to support our own souls. But we need very greatly to find for ourselves rest amid the perplexing controversies of the day, amid the fears and painful uncertainties of our own many questionings.

It is not now the time to go into systems of faith, or evidences of religious truth. But it is a gain to learn the mental condition through which we may best embrace God, and most reverently regard His revelation of Himself.

Most important it is for us to bear in mind, that the rest we need is to be acquired only by secret communing with God Himself. Elijah was not taken as many a prophet was, as his successor Elisha was, and before him Jonah, from a life of labour and free intercourse with the world. He had come forth, when we first read of him, from retirement, from some secret home in which he had dwelt with God. There, no doubt, he had learnt the first elements of rest and spiritual strength, in intimate communion with God, in quiet prayer, in communing with his own heart in his chamber and being still, as the true safeguard against the assaults of controversy and excitement. The groundwork of the faith needs to be laid deep in this the first principle of spiritual life. The energies of Elijah's strength were drawn out of this secret spring. His refuge, when life decayed, was to the same source. It is this that has ever been the formation and growth of all strong faith and saintliness. Who can count up the times of prayer, the seasons given to meditation on the things of God, which have characterized all who have been great in the service of God? To the active mind of a busy age, these seasons seem to be mere waste. But in them lies the spirit's secret stay, the power of rising above the attractions of the outer world, of overcoming spiritual evils within oneself, of producing any deep effect on the world around, of impressing on others higher truths, a purer example, a nobler standard of life. To hold one's ground against the influence of fashion, to turn the tide of a false popular opinion, to be able to resist the catching influences of loose habits of conversation, to stand alone and keep true to one's higher aims, and not be led to sink all in the excitement of the hour, — these efforts need a strength above the resources of genius, above any mere moral elevation of character. It is a strength nurtured in prayer, fed at the altar, gained slowly but surely by long, earnest, patient communing with God.

Moreover, a yet further strength, sufficient to support one standing alone, it may be, to be a witness for the right, the true, the noble, and the generous, in the face of the mean, the impure, the false, and the earthly— is to be found in that simple hold upon God, which seemed to be Elijah's one truth. One practical dogma formed Elijah's creed. His heart's deep fervour, the supernatural of his life, consisted virtually in one absorbed conviction. No other utterance of his is left behind him to which we can appeal to ascertain his faith, but the great truth in which he went forth on his mission, "If the Lord be God, follow Him." It was the strong grasp of a strong mind on this greatest spiritual truth, with nothing allowed to interrupt its influence, nothing to diminish its force, that formed Elijah's strength. And it must be so always. Whatever advance we make in spiritual life, whatever refinement through discipline we attain, whatever increase of knowledge is developed within us, the real strength of the character, the firmness and courage of the man, is just in proportion to the hold which this simple truth of the being and presence of God has upon his soul. The consciousness of what follows from it, what consistently ought to follow, if God be God, if the One Almighty Ruler of the creatures whom He hath made for His glory, have His rightful claim acknowledged, His right within each soul, the absolute sway which He demands, which surely is His due—it is this which is the soul's truest strength.

The rebelliousness of the will, the independence of spirit, the tampering with scepticism, the carelessness as to contact with evil, the laxity of conscience, the failing of reverence, and of the sense of duty,—which are the special sins of the day, are results of the loss of that hold upon the mind of the Presence of God. It is often observed how in earlier ages, in the freshness of man's life, this sense of God, when felt, was felt more keenly than in such a state as ours. The very development of intellect, the very increase and multiplicity of knowledge, seem to dim the conscience, and perplex the view of God. To gain Elijah's simple possession of the great truth in the strong zeal of a fresh faith, is the lesson above all to be pressed home as the moral of Elijah's history.

And this one truth in its simplicity pervades the Holy Scriptures even to the end. The perfection of the most advanced stage of spiritual life, is summed up in this conviction, even as the earliest precepts of Revelation were grounded upon it: "This is life eternal, to know Thee the only true God, and Jesus Christ, Whom Thou hast sent [b]." "All shall know Me, from the least to the greatest [c]." Such are the injunctions and the promises to God's elect which are found among His latest teachings. To know and to bear an unshaken witness to what we know in this simplicity of truth, is the call which specially the circumstances of our own times require; a call that, whatever our measure of knowledge may be, whatever our reach of mental power, will be the ground of our sentence, the test of our faithfulness in that Day, when He will arise to "give to every man according as his work shall be [d]."

[b] St. John xvii. 3.   [c] Heb. viii. 11.   [d] Rev. xxii. 12.

SERMON IX.

Elisha.

1 KINGS xix. 12—16.

"And after the earthquake a fire ; but the Lord was not in the fire : and after the fire a still small voice. And it was so, when Elijah heard it, that he wrapped his face in his mantle, and went out, and stood in the entering in of the cave. And behold, there came a voice unto him, and said, What doest thou here, Elijah ? And he said, I have been very jealous for the Lord God of hosts : because the children of Israel have forsaken Thy covenant, thrown down Thine altars, and slain Thy prophets with the sword ; and I, even I only, am left : and they seek my life, to take it away. And the Lord said unto him, Go, return on thy way to the wilderness of Damascus : and when thou comest, anoint Hazael to be king over Syria : And Jehu the son of Nimshi shalt thou anoint to be king over Israel : and Elisha the son of Shaphat of Abel-meholah shalt thou anoint to be prophet in thy room."

ONE of the great masters of fiction, who wrote at a time when it was thought higher praise to be true to nature than to administer degrading and outrageous stimulants, has spoken touchingly of the sadness of an auction. Those pieces of furniture are parts of a whole which make up what may be called the sacrament of home. They are separated from the associations which make them almost sacred ; from the well-known faces, the loving looks, the quick shadows cast upon them by the winter fire. Some coarse gibe is flung at them, and raises an unfeeling laugh. Something in this spirit are men too ready to deal with those bibles, which are the haunted homes of every Christian heart. They will not survey them as a whole. They will single out this or that incident, and treat it with a ribald wit, which vexes the hearts of God's children.

It is one of the advantages of a course of sermons like the present that it enables and invites the preacher to look at the career of one of the prophets as a great whole, and absolves him from the distasteful task of apologizing for this or that particular incident in it. It is my duty to-night to present to you the character of Elisha as a whole, and in his message to his time to catch those predictions which convey a message to our own time.

I. For the *character* of Elisha. Never was there a shallower reading of sacred history than that which would represent Elisha as a second Elijah, drawn by a feebler hand, and by a mythical imagination at a lower state of tension. He has, indeed, "a double portion" of his predecessor's spirit, that is, he is related to him as an eldest son. He is not a dwarfed and flaccid Elijah. The manifold and richly various wisdom of God[a] is stricken with no such harmony of creation in the natural or spiritual world. "The wall of the city has twelve foundations, and in them the names of the twelve apostles of the Lamb." But the twelve foundations are all different; sapphire and emerald, topaz and amethyst, each is beautiful, but with a dissimilar beauty. How different is St. Peter flinging himself into the waters, which are peoples and nations, from St. John calmly abiding in the ship. The Spirit of God has not exhausted all His tenderness in Augustine, nor all His eloquence in Taylor, nor all His thought in Butler. One mould is broken in a great teacher, and another is framed, more adapted to its day and work.

[a] ἡ πολυποίκιλος σοφία. Ephes. iii. 10.

And so Elisha is not a new Elijah. The "still small voice" of which we read, just before his call, is the emblem of the younger prophet. Gentleness is his characteristic; help, and deliverance, and salvation, are his work.

His very *name* signifies "God's Salvation." That name involves a blessed statement, which almost every action of his marvellous life might have recalled to the mind of his people. The last doings of his life, some of his last recorded words, possibly contain an allusion to it, "The arrow of the Lord's deliverance, and the arrow of deliverance from Syria [b]."

His *miracles* run on in rapid succession, until they have been called with over freedom the "Acts of Elisha," as if we were reading the legendary doings of some medieval saint. They are stamped with one peculiar and consistent impress. The very first is the merciful healing of the waters of Jericho. Among the last in the cluster which relates to the sons of the prophets is the feeding of the hundred with the twenty loaves [c], the faint prelude of the miracle in the Gospel for Refreshment Sunday.

There is something also in the *homeliness* of many of these miracles which contrasts with the mysterious awe that broods round the path which is trodden by the elder prophet. We may trace it in the restoration of the poor man's borrowed axe [d], in the oil that fills vessel after vessel, like water from some abundant spring [e]. Above all we may trace it in those fresh and tender pages, pathetic with a pathos that puts fiction and rhetoric to shame, in the history of the Shunammite.

Of course we cannot forget that in the history of

---

[b] 2 Kings xiii. 17.   [c] Ibid. iv. 42.   [d] Ibid. iii. 6.
[e] Ibid. iv. 5, 6.

Elisha moments come, when God's glory and the good of His people demand a sterner dealing; when the gentle prophet of salvation must utter the truth that burns, or even wield the weapon that destroys. Yet, even in these cases, we seem to feel as if he had been breathing in an alien element. After that terrible incident, that one miracle of destruction which punished the guilty parents of a guilty town, and perhaps saved the forty-two who perished from a deeper sin and more dreadful punishment; after that solemn curse in the name of the Lord; the thought seems to press upon the prophet's loving heart. He must have time to recover: he must bathe his fevered brow in the lonely air, and breathe in the mountain solitude. "And there came forth two she bears out of the wood, and tare forty and two of them. *And he went from thence to Mount Carmel*, and from thence he returned to Samaria[f]." In the campaign of the three kings against Moab, he speaks with unwonted, yet surely not with unbecoming wrath. We hear once again the mighty voice of Elijah: "As the Lord of Hosts liveth, before whom I stand, surely, were it not that I regard the presence of Jehoshaphat the king of Judah, I would not look toward thee, nor see thee[g]." Yet it would appear as if he doubted whether the calm vision of God might pass across the mirror of a spirit that had been clouded by the hot breath of human anger. And he calls for sacred music to allay his perturbation. One, and one only could be angry, and yet contract no more defilement than the lucid water from sweeping over a bed of stainless marble.

He is no cloistered ascetic, no head of the Carmelite brothers, no monk of the Old Testament. It cannot

---

[f] 2 Kings ii. 24, 25.   [g] Ibid. iii. 14; cf. 1 Kings xvii. 1.

be truly said by any of these, *Elisseus noster.* Ascetic his little chamber may be, with bed, and table, and stool, and candlestick; ascetic compared with the clubrooms, where scientific luxury gives you the most comfortable seat, and the most feathered footfall, and the best-dressed dinners upon the most economical principle, where you can live like a noble upon little more than the income of a clerk, and learn the art of the graceful and systematic selfishness that has the softest voice and the hardest heart. Ascetic it may be, compared with rooms in this place, (unless Oxford be much changed,) where luxury and extravagance are to be found that may help to break the strong heart of some self-denying parent. But in Elisha the practical and the contemplative are exquisitely balanced. "Carmel fits him for Samaria, and Samaria for Carmel." There seems to be some special attraction which draws him to towns. "If Elijah," it has been said, "enters a city, it is only to deliver his message of fire, and be gone. Elisha, on the other hand, is an inhabitant of cities[h]." He is found in the campaign of the kings of Israel, Judah, and Edom[i]; for even in an army the everlasting Presence can go forth with us, and fill us with unfailing peace. He pauses in the Shunammite's house, as if he loved to hear the stream of family life rippling beside him, and to feel its spray upon his face[k]. For he has no unworthy fear that he will lose dignity or influence by the curious, and not always kindly, inspection of intimacy. There is one great difference between the works of nature and of art. The latter, however gentle and graceful they

[h] Mr. Grove's Article on Elisha in "Dictionary of the Bible." See 2 Kings ii. 18, 25; v. 32; vi. 32, 24; vi. 14; v. 9, 24; vi. 32; xiii. 17.
[i] 2 Kings iii. 11.   [k] Ibid. iv. 10.

may appear to the naked eye, when looked at under the microscope exhibit coarseness and want of consummate finish. The delicate lace-work is a collection of lines that have the rigidity of wire. But the minutest piece of God's workmanship, leaf, or feather, or beetle's wing, is soft and exquisite to the lowest point at which we can trace it down the abyss of littleness. And so an unreal spiritual life, a hollow morality, an adventitious holiness, looks coarse and ugly under the microscope of intimacy. How many preachers are there whom it is better not to know! O for the quiet unpretending holiness which grows upon us as we inspect it; of which, as its possessor passes by oft, and turns in to eat bread, men and women are constrained to say, "I perceive that this is an holy man of God which passeth by us continually." For such, intimacy is not inconsistent with the unstudied dignity that will neither cringe to a patron, nor bow before the great and honourable, borne, like Naaman, in chariots.

To complete the view of Elisha's character. He is full of the most refined *humanity*. He can recognise in an afflicted woman the feelings that are too deep for words, because the loving God, the maker of the subtly-chorded instrument, has reserved their music for Himself. He can sympathise with a conscience at once weak and scrupulous. He can bear patiently with the long-continued cross of a weak and unprincipled attendant, who cannot understand his purity and self-denial. He loves to appear with good news, to assure the childless woman that a little babbling voice shall yet make music in her home, to tell the besieged, whose carrion-fare costs them so dear, that the abundance of the harvest shall yet be poured upon them, as if from the windows of heaven. The fuller morality of the Gospel makes us exacting. We criticise holy men of old by the purer and more searching light which we possess. We sometimes claim from them a chivalry which they do not possess. Shall we forget that answer, worthy of the gentlest record of Christian chivalry, "Thou shalt not smite them. Wouldest thou smite those whom thou hast taken captive with thy sword and with thy bow?"

Consider, too, how deeply, how almost passionately, with what surpassing human love, he can love his sombre and awful master. "My father, my father! the chariots of Israel, and the horsemen thereof. And he took hold of his own clothes, and rent them in two pieces." Glorious as is that departure of Elijah, we yet feel that there is in it something of the sorrow that clings to the partings of mortality. It is a radiant sunset, but there is a trouble round about it. Even here, where there are so many young men present, there must be some who know how last looks are graven upon the memory. Once, and once only, did a separation for life between loving hearts leave joy behind it. It was after the stone had been rolled away from the sepulchre, when the great Forty Days were over, and the risen Lord was taken up in the cloud out of sight. "And they returned to Jerusalem with great joy." *With joy*, because evermore there dwelt with them the memory of the pierced Hands that were lifted up to bless. But here, at the ascension of Elijah, we see of how much love and sorrow the prophet was capable.

II. We now consider the message to this age which is conveyed in Elisha's message to his own age.

1. The first, and not the least important of these, is directly connected with his *prophetic office.* Let us

first form to ourselves a clear notion of that office in general, and of Elisha's peculiar relation to it. The lesson which we are seeking will then follow without effort.

(*a.*) I need, perhaps, scarcely caution you against that restricted view of the prophet's office, which would make him simply a *foreteller* of future events. He is, indeed, that, and especially in reference to the sufferings of Christ, and the glory that shall follow. Dim, indeed, and mysterious are the images of the Sufferer with pale and dying lips, and of the risen King. Yet as we know some shape in a mirror in the grey winter morning, because we have known it before by seeing it a hundred times in the broad daylight; so we recognise Christ in the clear obscure of prophecy, because we have seen Him in the sunlight of the Gospels. If we have no Messianic prophecy falling from the lips of Elisha, yet we find that he can read the future; that he can see the absent; that he can pierce the veil of flesh which hangs between his soul and that of other men; that he can peruse the bloody lines of Hazael's face, and read the story of his life by a supernatural light.

But the idea of the Nàbi is not to be limited to that of the foreseer or foreteller. The root from which it comes denotes that which jets or boils up, and comes forth with precipitate motion. It means an interpreter between God and man, who in words that well and gush forth, foretells future events, or unfolds divine mysteries, or enforces everlasting moral laws. The Greek word προφήτης with its double meaning of *foretelling* and *annunciation* is no inadequate rendering.

We should also remember that the prophets of Israel are to be divided into two eras. In the first we have their historical action, in the second we have their writings. There are prophets who have never penned their inspiration. The era of unwritten prophecy ends with Elijah and Elisha in the tenth and ninth centuries before Christ. The era of written prophecy has been divided by modern critics, the enemies of the theocracy, as Syro-Assyrian, Chaldean, and Persian.

Now you will remember that in the era of the unwritten prophets, to which Elisha belongs, the prophet is mainly this, the interpreter of God, "the organ of all that is most pure and loving in the popular conscience," the solemn witness against wrong, the remembrancer of right. His office is the inverse of that which modern statesmen claim for themselves. They claim to be the exponents of the popular will, and thus to enjoy the privilege of being always on the winning side. But the prophet of old is the stern opponent of popular or royal will, and is always for a time on the losing side.

And unbelief now does not fail to whisper what was doubtless said by their contemporaries. Impracticable men! their zeal becomes fanaticism. Their fidelity to unpopular principles degenerates into narrowness. Living for an ideal, they exact that which is impossible from men who live in the regions of reality. Troublesome Puritans whom their enthusiasm renders incorruptible, and who on religious questions will listen only to the inexorable logic of a truth which they believe to be divine.

Brethren, though we be not prophets, nor prophets' sons, we need something of this part of the prophetic spirit ; we need to remember Elisha in Dothan.

The character of Englishmen seems to have altered strangely in the last twenty years. They used to believe and construct; they now doubt and destroy. They used to be quiet and practical; they are now a restless race, a horde of minute philosophers. Intellectual modesty was the characteristic of our more distinguished students. One hears now of vain and clever young men, who tell the world that Descartes and Leibnitz, Plato and Aristotle, do not answer to their thought; that Bishop Butler is not a philosopher, and Augustine deficient in the critical faculties, and that the Gospels are not so spiritual as a new Gospel which they patronise. It was the characteristic of an indomitable race never to know when it was beaten. Its characteristic now seems to be that it should always know when it is beaten, and give up in time. We have arrived at moral and political pantheism. We believe in laws of society working out the will of the majority by a fatality that cannot be resisted. We fold our hands, and say each one, "We must submit. What am I, but a single grain of sand? Can I heave up the mountain which is above me?" Ah, brethren, a million "I wills" cannot make a single "I ought." From voices which are local, though they rise from a nation, and transitory, though they are pronounced by a generation, we must look up with the prophets to the everlasting right. And still, as in the beleaguered city of the Church we are tempted to swell the faithless cry, "Alas, how shall we do?" we should pray for opened eyes, that we may see the horses and chariots of fire, stretching in unending line from the feeble wall to the steps of God's throne, and filling the mountain with the splendour of their presence.

2. There are other lessons which Elisha seems to announce to our time, and which may be readily indicated.

(*a.*) A warning against the spirit of mockery, so prevalent among the young.

Nothing so unsuitable to youth, the season for reverence and admiration.

We of this day want something to admire. We may have grown wise, but a mocking Mephistophelic spirit walks by our side. Some flaw in every gem, some speck in every fruit, something base in every apparent virtue, some selfish sediment in every apparent self-denial; some physical or moral defect, some baldness upon the head of every prophet or man of God (perhaps the mark of the circlet of the crown of thorns) which makes you meet his solemn voice with some contemptuous cry.

We may also find a warning against two spiritual evils of vast extent upon opposite sides.

(β.) A warning against the spirit of irregularity in religion. If ever there were men who might have claimed to have been above rules in religion, they were these prophets of Israel. Why they were raised up in the ten tribes mainly to supply to the faithful people of Israel a substitute for the Church from which they were unavoidably severed. Yet see how Elijah upon Carmel offers up his prayer in communion with the Church "at the time of the offering of the evening sacrifice." See how Elisha's prayer brings down the thunder-burst upon the far hills of Moab "in the morning, when the meat-offering was offered." So all faithful hearts keep time with the great pulsation of the Church's mighty heart.

(γ.) A warning against the opposite spirit of formality.

This is conveyed by an incident in connection with Gehazi[1]. Who and what was he? one of those men

[1] 2 Kings iv. 29—31.

so often met with, living upon the surface of society, an outward superficial existence, touched by religion upon the surface, not at the centre of their being, a sort of spiritual Boswell or Eckermann, pleased to gain consequence for himself by his connection with Elisha. Bear with me if in Gehazi carrying the staff I see the very type of some young *dilettante* priest, going from a university to his parish. Gehazi bore the prophet's staff, and laid it upon that pale face, and he expects that it will flush again with the glow of life. It was not a dead staff that was wanted. It was a living man with God's living spirit in his heart. A young man thinks that he will introduce this or that service, this or that change. He will borrow this from Herbert, or that from Suckling, or that from some Church which he has admired. It may be well. But you want something more than a dead thing which has belonged to a prophet. The virtue is in the grasp. You want the knowledge gained in the schools of the prophets, and the chastening self-denial, and the earnest communions. And you must hold strongly the one staff which is long enough to knock at the gate of heaven. And you must breathe your own very living breath down into those dead souls; so only they shall live.

I know not whether it may seem over-fanciful, if I add that two other warnings seem to be conveyed, one by the first miracle of Elisha, the other by the latest incident of his life.

(δ.) A warning against over-addiction to old modes of conveying religious truth.

Of this great Church of ours it may be said, "The situation of the city is pleasant." And yet at this moment, when currents from "welling fountain-heads of change" are streaming over to us, and meeting in the denial of the very preamble of religion, in the negative of the supernatural and of a personal God, must we not add, "From these waters there is death, and barren land?" And what shall heal them? Nothing but the old salt, the old Creed, and the old Gospel; only as we reverently place the sacramental wine in a golden cup, so let the bread be given in the best and choicest vehicle which our labour can frame. Does not the prophet cry, "Bring me a new cruse?"

(ε.) A warning against trusting in new and sublimated forms of Christian thought.

In that incident in 2 Kings xiii., it was the hand of an old man, nearly ninety years of age; it was a weak and withered hand. But if the Prophet's hand had not been on the sinewy hand of the young king, the bow had been drawn in vain. So this Creed that has no form or comeliness, this Book which some would have us believe to be but an old and withered Jew's hand, must be on the bow that shall shoot the arrow of our deliverance from the enemies of the human spirit.

III. Brethren, in this our day there will not be wanting those who will smile at Augustine's favourite thought. How the dead child figured our fallen humanity dead in Adam. How the staff laid upon the pale cold face, "but there was neither voice nor hearing," shewed that the Law could never give life. How the great eternal God came to him who was little, the Saviour to him who was to be saved, the living to the dead. How He contracted His greatness, and fitted Himself to our littleness, that He might make the body of our vileness like the body of His glory. How He signified all the impotence of the law in the staff, all His loving-kindness, and compassion, and sympathy, in Elisha. But if we shrink from this as mystical, in one point, as Christians, we shall agree. No single type fully represents Him. But all these isolated types of moral beauty in king, or priest, or prophet, find their centre in the incarnate God. And "the still small voice" of Bethlehem and Calvary, of the shrouded glory, and the miracles of compassion, and the broken heart; and the gentleness of Elisha, which is so human and domestic, so tender and so strong; leads us on toward the gentle Humanity of Him who is meek and lowly in heart. To Him may you all come for pardon, for sympathy. There are strange possibilities in the future. A man of genius has recorded that once in his youth, in a vision he saw a haggard man turn and look upon him with a face of hatred. At last he saw that it was *himself* twenty years older, himself with the fatal lines of dissipation ploughed into his face. Who, indeed, in a congregation like this, can imagine the difference between the gay young man and "the grey and gap-toothed old man, lean as death?" May you be saved from this. May you prepare yourselves each to lay one stone of that pyramid, of which each generation plants one course in the shadow, waiting for the eternal morning to strike upon the topmost row.

SERMON X.

Job.

JOB xiii. 15.

"Though He slay me, yet will I trust in Him."

RESPECTING the general character of the Book of Job, the opinions of critics and philosophers have exhibited a remarkable unanimity. One calls it "the Melchizedec among the Old Testament books;" another says of it, "that it hovered like a meteor over the old Hebrew literature, in it, but not of it; ... never alluded to, and scarcely ever quoted, till at last the light which it had heralded rose up full over the world in Christianity." Yet a third (one of the most eminent amongst modern philosophers) remarks concerning its hero,—"Job, maintaining his virtue, and justifying the utterance of the Creator respecting him, sits upon his heap of ashes, as the pride and glory of God.... He conquers, and his victory is a triumph beyond the stars! Be it history, be it poetry, he who thus wrote was a Divine Seer!"

Of such a Book as this, breathing a spirit thus lofty and majestic, and carrying on its forefront the visible imprint of Divine inspiration, the question of the age and authorship is one of but secondary consequence.

Two things, however, seem to be almost universally

admitted. First, that the hero of the Book, whenever he lived, was not its author; and secondly, that the Book was written long after the days of Moses, and long before the period of the exile.

Further than this I should deem it inexpedient (as it is certainly unnecessary) to speculate, but for two considerations. First, because it adds greatly to the interest and significance of a book, if we can determine, even approximately, the circumstances under which it was written; and secondly, because, with the critical direction I have indicated, such approximate determination seems far from difficult. If, indeed, it be allowed that the Book was written between the death of Moses and the period of the exile, the epoch towards which we are irresistibly led, as that of its probable composition, is the great age of David and Solomon. In that period, the people of Israel, almost at a single bound, passed from the condition of a loose fraternity of lawless clans to that of a powerful heroic monarchy. Nor when we read the Book of Psalms does this brilliant transformation appear any longer inexplicable. For there we are smitten at once by that mighty wing-stroke of spiritual power which bore Israel aloft in a single generation to the height of a commanding secular dominion, and of a world-wide spiritual ascendancy.

But all the more, therefore, do we look anxiously for the breaking forth of this spiritual power in the direction of intellectual speculation. Has the spirit of Israel force enough to construct a monarchy, and to create the hymnody of all time? and can we suppose, that when confronted with the terrible problems of action and existence, it will have no power to stimulate the intellect to their consideration? Mighty in action and devotion, can it be impotent in thought alone?

It may be deemed by some a sufficient answer to this question to point to the recognised literature of the days of Solomon—to the practical wisdom of the Proverbs, and the *vanitas vanitorum* of the Preacher. But yet, excellent, and even necessary, as are these products of pious prudence and worldly experience for the completion of Divine wisdom, few can have failed to feel that they march, at best, with unequal step beside the rapt and lofty spirit of the Psalms. It is not in the strong bright secular satisfaction of the practical moralist, it is not in the weary dissatisfaction of the palled pleasure-seeker, who, having played experiments with life and failed, has only strength to tell his own sad tale as a warning to mankind, it is not in these that we can match the profound spiritual emotion, the awful moral earnestness, of the Psalms. We want something as wide in the sweep of its thought as the Psalms in the range of their feeling; something which, like them, shall sound the utmost depth of our fears, and soar to the utmost height of our aspirations; which, like them, shall be as spiritual as it is wise, as strong as it is tender; and that we meet with what we seek nowhere in the whole range of inspired philosophy but in the Book of Job, this surely (taken in connexion with the critical conclusions I have mentioned) furnishes a presumption of no inconsiderable force, that for the age of its author we must look to the great days of the undivided kingdom.

One thing, however, is certain, that whether written in those days or not, the Book of Job is at least worthy of them.

Passing on now to inquire into the central purpose of the Book, we soon discover that it is the object of the writer to discuss a question which, from its interest, no less than its obscurity, has been the subject of debate and anxiety in all ages;—What, viz., is the precise connexion between sin and suffering? A question which loses itself, in turn, in the still more mysterious inquiry, How could a God of love permit the existence of evil?

In order to give precision and reality to this inquiry, the author avails himself of the existing and well-known history of Job. Avoiding merely abstract inquiries, which would have presented little of interest and less of profit, he states, in the simplest and briefest manner, the facts of the Patriarch's life. Born in Arabia, in patriarchal days, Job was a just man, and devout, fearing God and loving his neighbour. The story of his earlier life is a delightful picture of pastoral simplicity, domestic affection, and pious prosperity; of wealth employed to promote the reasonable happiness of its human owners, and sanctified by the continual remembrance of the Divine Giver. The only drawback is, that this godly home is built upon the earth; is reared above the beating of a fiery subterranean heart, which, as experience too sadly testifies, may at any time shake it into ruins by the mighty fever-throb of some spiritual earthquake.

In the ordinary case we know of such catastrophes only that they have occurred, but here we are permitted to witness the gradual accumulation of those hidden forces which are to be the terrible agents of ruin. We get a glimpse of that spiritual world, which, arching above us, on the one hand, as a bright beneficent heaven of Divine love—on the other stretches deep beneath the thin crust of our mortal existence into those dark and secret abysses where the volcanic forces of moral evil lie stored.

Satan appears in heaven to question Job's piety, and to suggest that he serves God only for what he can gain by it. In answer to this malicious suggestion, the

Accuser is permitted to deprive him first of property, then of children, and then of bodily health and comfort, till at length, stripped of all which had made life dear and precious, the stricken patriarch seats himself amongst the ashes, naked and destitute, his body corrupted by the awful black leprosy of Arabia, and his miserable spirit darkened throughout the whole circuit of its heaven by the storm-cloud of his unparalleled woes.

And yet "in all this," we are told, "Job sinned not, nor charged God foolishly." Deprived of a fortune which had no parallel in the East, he answers never a word. Stricken in a more vulnerable place by the death of his children, he pours forth the fulness of his chastened spirit in the sublimest words of resignation which ever fell from the lips of a mourner; and even when cast down upon the ashes, in the prostration of a mortal and disgusting sickness, he exclaims only, in the meekness and calmness of a self-possession strong and sublime enough to have dignified a throne, "shall we receive good at the hands of the Lord, and shall we not receive evil?"

Satan then was sufficiently answered. It was proved already that at least his accusations were false, and accordingly he disappears altogether from the scene convicted and vanquished.

Job is left alone with his afflictions; to sustain their burden and ponder their meaning in the light of such truth as he possessed.

Now it was a doctrine of that age and country (a doctrine not without an element of truth, and one naturally growing up in a primitive form of life), that God proportioned a man's sufferings to the heinousness of his personal transgressions. If this doctrine were true in the case of Job, it plainly proved that he was a perfect monster of iniquity. But the author has already allowed us to see that this is not the fact; and therefore we must look upon the case of Job as a conclusive refutation of the popular Arabian theory.

Perhaps, if the patriarch had been left in peace, he might have attained to this conclusion without any severe internal conflict. But matters were ordered otherwise. He was visited by three of his friends— men pious, upright, and had in reputation, who had met together by appointment "to mourn with him and to comfort him." Approaching him at first with the tenderest and sincerest sympathy, they are yet impelled, by the very orthodoxy of their views, to bring him to a sense of (as they conclude) his extraordinary guilt. According to the popular doctrine (which Job had hitherto believed no less than they) God could justly inflict suffering only on account of sin. If, then, suffering existed, they must either assume that its subject was a sinner, or that God was unjust. But to pious men the latter was, of course, an impossible supposition, and the more clearly they saw this, the more precisely were they prepared to affirm the alternative.

On the other hand, the patriarch knew that this assumption of theirs was untrue. Of his own moral rectitude, or at least of the sincerity and whole-heartedness of his endeavour after moral rectitude, he had the most indubitable evidence which a man can possess, viz., that of his own inward experience. Of the trustworthiness of this experience he was all the more convinced in proportion to the extravagance of the friends' assumption; for they were logically bound to affirm, and did affirm, not only that Job was a sinner, but that he was one of the most notorious sinners who ever lived. This Job utterly denied. A sinner he was, and was ready to admit that he was; but a sinner whose iniquity was enormous in comparison with that of his fellow-men he was not, and would not acknowledge himself to be.

This honesty of Job, his friends regarded as spiritual hardness and hypocrisy, and met it with an ever-increasing harshness of accusation which did but increase the sufferer's anguish and deepen his perplexity. Much could be said on the side of the friends, and all that could be said for them is urged with the utmost possible force. And hence the great difficulty of perceiving at a superficial glance the error of the friends, and the justice of the patriarch's complaints against them. All upon their part is so correctly conceived, and so justly, eloquently (even sublimely), expressed, that it requires the closest attention to detect what is false or exaggerated therein; while again, on the part of Job, all is at first so chaotic and impassioned, so wildly daring in thought, so carelessly impetuous (almost to blasphemy) in expression, that it is difficult (at least for a western mind) to follow the development of his feeling and faith. On a closer study, however, of the Book, all this is reversed; and the more it is studied, the more one's admiration grows of the vast range of its thought, of the deep fervour of its inspiration, even of the consummate art of its construction.

Bend over that turbulent chaotic mind of Job, and you will perceive at length, seething in its fiery depths, the elements of a new creation. Sift and analyze, on the other hand, the eloquent commonplaces of his friends, and in their application, at least, you will find them as unfruitful as they are false.

The friends turn about everywhere within the narrow circle of their original syllogism. Personal suffering is the punishment of personal sin. Job suffers; therefore he has sinned. That is the whole. Words are multiplied, illustration is piled upon illustration, and metaphor on metaphor, with an inexhaustibleness truly oriental, but of progress or variety in thought there is absolutely nothing. There is one narrow dogma. It is defended on different grounds ; now on that of revelation, again on that of tradition, and still again on that of personal experience—but the thing, the *doctrine*, never once enlarges, or even alters in the process.

Again it is passed through different minds : through that of Eliphaz, the grave and dignified patriarchal chieftain, the man of practical wisdom and large charity ; through that of Bildad, the man of precedent and tradition, distrustful of talent and apprehensive of change ; finally, through that of Zophar, the passionate and unreasoning conservative, narrow in his conceptions, bitter, and sometimes even coarse and offensive, in his invective. The minds are different, through which the one doctrine is passed, and they tinge it with their own colour in the passage, but of other change it suffers absolutely nothing. Urged, now tenderly as in the first controversy, now furiously as in the second, and now doggedly and uncharitably as in the third, it is still the same narrow, hard, uncompromising dogma—the dead weight of unelastic authority which presses on the writhing and struggling spirit of the patriarch with the pitiless persistence of an unchanging condemnation.

Now it is out of the terrible struggle thus produced in the heart of Job, as he storms forth for light and comfort from this prison of condemnation, first in one direction and then in another, now in the form of complaint, now of appeal, and now again of believing triumph, that the life and sufferings of the patriarch yield up to us their instruction. Tried beyond endurance by his own inward perplexity, and the solemn blundering of his friends, he is driven to appeal from time to eternity, from the God of a rigid *lex talionis*, to the God who is just even to the suffering. Thrust back by his friends, he clings to God; and thrust back (as it seems) by God, he soars away above time and its prejudices to a higher truth and a better world.

Job's faith in the popular doctrine has been shattered against his own bitter experience. And now, feeling out anxiously in the darkness, he discovers three particulars, with respect to which it has become matter of imperative necessity that he shall get new light. First, as to the meaning of human suffering; secondly, as to the duration of human existence; and thirdly, as to the true character of God.

First, the old doctrine affirmed that personal suffering always meant personal sin; but this Job knew to be false, not only through the teaching of his own experience, but through observation of the course of the world. It was not only the guilty, but far more frequently the helpless, who suffered; it was not only the righteous, but very frequently, at least, the notoriously wicked who prospered. Job urged these facts with a point and force which ought to have extorted, at least, concession from his adversaries; and when they still persist in urging their terrible accusation, with even more bitter asperity, he does not hesitate to charge them with cowardice and hypocrisy.

> "Will you speak what is wrong for God? (he cries)
> Will you talk deceitfully for Him?
> Will you accept His person?
> Or play the part of God's advocates?"

You plead (as you imagine) for God, and yet you know that your heart trembles within you while you plead. You say that there is no doubt, and you know that there is. You say that it is monstrous to call in question this judgment which has befallen me; and you know that you yourselves have only not questioned the like because you dare not. There *is* difficulty, there is mystery, there is the appearance of injustice; and do you think you can do God honor by denying that which is? Were it a man's doing you would call it in question, but, because it is God's, and He is great, you accept His person, you favor Him, you wink at His questionable doings; you say that that is right in Him which you don't think to be right in itself, which you would declare to be wrong in another.

No doubt God is right! I believe that far more profoundly than you do; but the action which we attribute to Him (you and I), viz. that He has punished me for my sins, that is not right! You say it is out of a partial favoring of God, but I, on the contrary, who know that God would hate to be favored, to be called right at the expense of being thought wrong, I dare not imitate you. Nor can I even be content to be silent, or to drown the fatal whisper of doubt in loud-voiced hollow obsequiousness. No! I want light, I want deliverance, I want peace; and if in seeking these I must needs perish, lo! I take my life in my hands, and freely offer it up as the sacrifice. He may slay me; I may be consumed in the kindling of His anger, even as the insect is extinguished in the flame, but yet, though He slay me, even then will I trust in Him and wait for His salvation.

Words over bold, perhaps, for a frail mortal, but words as real and pathetic as ever were thrown up out of the depths of a suffering and passionate heart; words which breathe and burn and live; which make us feel the living heart throbbing beneath them, or rather pouring itself forth upon them, in a real masterful wrestling with God. Would God, my brethren, we met the difficulties of our own day with an honesty as determined, and a faith as confident as that of Job. Would God that we had in our hearts ever such a spark or scintilla of his heaven-compelling earnestness, even though at the cost of ten times his boldness of speech. For it is not the word that God notices in our prayers, but the impassioned and spirit-driven soul which is yearning and struggling to find Him; which, having seized the outstretched hand of His love, refuses to loosen its hold for all the terrors and lightning of Omnipotence, crying with Jacob "I will not let Thee go, unless Thou bless me;" yea, with Job, "I will trust Thee though Thou slay me."

But we remarked in the second place, that the rejection of the popular doctrine opened up another possibility in connexion with the future. That doctrine (declaring the earthly life of man to be a rounded and self-explanatory whole) left it possible to take a dreary view of theology, such a view of it as is expressed by Job in the seventh chapter and elsewhere. But if our earthly life did not present this imaginary moral completeness (and that it did not was to Job self-evident), then the question might be started, whether perhaps there might not be wider spaces of time, and freer conditions of existence, in which the tangled beginnings of our life might be worked out, through a gradual unravelling, to more beautiful and comprehensible issues. The idea which was thus left possible to Job gradually took more and more definite shape. It comes up in the fourteenth chapter as a mere conception, in the sixteenth as a demand, and at length, in the nineteenth, as a confident and triumphant belief. Very suddenly does the celestial afflatus descend on the patriarch's spirit at last, but yet we can already discern, I think, in the saddening, pleading tone of verse 21, that some great change is at hand.

"Have pity on me," cries the sufferer, "have pity on me, O ye my friends, for the hand of Eloah hath touched me." These words seem to bespeak that softening of the heart into an unusual tenderness; that strange fusion of the feelings into an inexplicable yearning mobility, into an exceeding sensitiveness and apprehensiveness, which so strikingly precedes the ecstatic rapture of some conversions. One who knew anything of this condition of spirit, and had watched narrowly the successive phases of Job's feeling, might almost have anticipated that sudden check, and sob as it were, of exultation with which at length he bursts forth.

"Oh that my words were written in a book, with an iron pen, graven in the rock for ever!" Ye may revile, misunderstand, distrust me, but I know that my Redeemer (my Vindicator) liveth; and as the Last one whose word (and not yours) shall be decisive, He shall arise for me upon the dust in which I have mouldered away, and vindicate my innocence; yea, and after my skin, now torn to pieces by disease, and without my flesh (which is nothing better than a torture and burden to me), I shall stand up in the presence of my Divine Avenger, "whom mine eyes shall behold, and not another." Thus, out of the dark night of Job's sorrow, there had shone forth for him the bright day-spring of immortality. He had seen it like a vision of Paradise; he had felt it like a breathing of the Blessed; he had heard it like a murmur of angels' songs; like the whisper of a hope, so full of love and holiness, that it must needs have come forth from the very heart of God.

And thus ever is sorrow the ministering priest which

lights the dark taper of truth in the arcanum of the spiritual sanctuary. The heart lies often dull and voiceless in the meaner satisfaction of a mere earthly prosperity, like an æolian lyre unstrung. But then the loose strings of feeling are gathered into the hand of affliction ; they are drawn tight into the straining sensitive tension of pain ; and lo ! every breath of heaven, as it sweeps along, draws from them divinest music.

Job's heart had been strained to such painful spiritual sensitiveness, that it responded, in wailing sadness, to every touch of the Breath of God. But, anon, there came the sound to him, as at Pentecost, of a mighty rushing wind, and as it swept across the sorrow-tuned heart, waking its fullest and deepest vibrations, there rung forth into the heaven such glorious chords—so full of a triumphant and majestic sweetness, that the very angels might have bent down to listen from the shadow of the heavenly throne. It was the first articulate utterance of the blessed hope of immortality.

But now, lastly, there was opened, in the rejection of the popular explanation, the third and grandest question of all ; viz., what was to be concluded, under the new conditions of thought, about the nature and character of God ?

The old doctrine had conceived of the Divine Justice as a something merely judicial ; as a quality which dispensed in this world (with even-handed impartiality) earthly rewards to the good, and earthly punishments to the evil. That was not true. But, then, what was true ? Something better ? or something worse ? That God was unjust ? or only that this was a mean and narrow conception of the nature of His justice ?

In this new disorder and divergence of the patriarch's thoughts — in this decisive separation of the hitherto single current of his devout feelings into two divergent streams—there would seem almost to arise for him the image of two Gods, the God of the old time and the God of the new ; the God of whose injustice he complained, and the God to whom he appealed for vindication. A duality involving that seeming contradiction between justice and love which only the sacrifice of the Cross could abolish.

And hence there follows (from this peculiarity in his spiritual position) that striking, almost startling, resemblance between Job and the suffering Messiah which a man must almost be blind to overlook. For Job is the innocent man, suffering as if he were guilty, for the confusion of Satan and the glory of God. Men cannot see this, and so they misapprehend and revile him, adding thus a deeper poignancy to his anguish, and forcing forth from him utterances of woe which are almost repeated word for word in the passion cries of the Psalms and Gospels. "They have gaped upon me with their mouth," he cries ; "they have smitten me upon the cheek reproachfully ;" "he hath made me a by-word of the people." Expressions which, I need not remind you, find their exact counterpart in the Passion Psalms and the Messianic portions of Isaiah.

To this outward coincidence of expression there corresponds, as we might have expected, a striking inward coincidence of spiritual experiences.

Job suffered so poignantly, because there was laid upon his consciousness the burden of a sin which was not his, and which did not seem natural to him. Had he deserved the wrath of God, he would have felt a certain fitness in its incidence ; would have crouched under it, most likely as the hardened do, in sullen defiance or abject fear. But now it was not so. He loved God, and yet God looked away from him; he was comparatively innocent, and yet he was thrust forth into the outer darkness and companionship of the ungodly. It was this incongruity which distressed him. It was his own horror of sin which gave the sting to its imputation; it was his own ardent love of God which gave to the withdrawal of God's love its bitterness.

It is this circumstance which makes Job's experience so highly typical and instructive; for though it be common enough for men to stand consciously beneath the frown of God, it is not common for them to do so with the bright assurance and undimmed spiritual sensitiveness of conscious innocence.

Of course the type falls infinitely short of the antitype; for even as Job's holiness and love of the Father came short of his Saviour's, even so greatly, so almost infinitely, did his sense of identity with the world's sin, and consequent subjection to the Divine wrath.

But still, however great the distinction, we may be enabled, I think (by throwing on the type the light of the antitype), to discern at once the solution of all Job's perplexities, and the deepest lesson of his life.

For thus we are enabled to perceive that God's Justice is an attribute, not merely which doles out gifts to the good, but which seeks to transform all men into its own likeness. Justice seeking to revenge itself; that was the old, bad, inadequate idea even of Christian men. Justice, seeking to make all men just; Justice, preparing the possibility of this through the honoring of the law in its own vicarious sufferings; Justice, going forth in the message of the Cross, and working in men the remorse of a just hatred of sin. That is the Redeeming Justice of our God and Father in Christ Jesus. And that Justice can inflict pain in mercy. It can inflict physical suffering to break down an apathetic animal indifference ; it can inflict inward remorse to make sin hateful and abhorrent ; yea, it can inflict suffering to be borne vicariously for the good of others ; for it knows that its chosen ministers, its consecrated priests, those who stand nearest the vision, waiting with straining ears for the whisper from within, will rejoice, like their Divine Master, to take up the Cross for the salvation of the world.

Oh! to be the crystal pavement beneath Christ's feet of flame ! to be the living bridge of pain He crosses by in passing forth from the outward heaven to the inward spirit of the lost ; to be the medium of throbbing flesh and blood, which transmits, through the anguish of its own nerve-thrill, the electric spark of life to the spiritually paralyzed and dead. This is to go up to Calvary to the Master ; it is to catch upon the pale fevered brow the very glory of Paradise ; it is to realize that grandest truth that "to serve God and to love Him is higher and better than happiness, though it be with wounded feet and bleeding brows, and hearts loaded with sorrow."

And, my brethren, however unfamiliar this thought may be to some of us, does it not express a state of soul which ought to be that of every living Christian ? If we live at all, we live through a personal participation of that very life of Christ which He sanctified through suffering. And if so, must it not necessarily follow, that every real Christian will experience the fundamental impulses of that life, and display its characteristic properties ; that there will be found in him a mode of feeling and action corresponding (in however low a degree) to every mode of feeling and action displayed by the Divine Master Himself?

True, we cannot offer a satisfactory atonement to God,

as Christ our Master did ; and yet we can feel, we ought to feel, that same self-sacrificing love which moved Him to offer one. We may not be able, with a love deeper than that of the Swiss patriot, to bury the whole spearsheaf of the Divine fury in our single heart ; but if we be Christians we can at least feel the rapture of the redeeming Passion which prompted that unparalleled sacrifice.

Is there a plague in the land, a plague of spiritual ignorance and indifference, of spiritual formalism and doubt, of fleshly pride and sensuality ? Are the black arrows of that pestilence destroying their thousands of every class and age, until, to the seeing eye, the streets and squares, yea, the homes and churches, of our guilty cities are filled with the ghastly heaps of the dying and dead ? Then, my young friends, if you have the fearless spirit within you of Christ's atoning, propitiating love, you will not steal aside into some safe spiritual covert where the danger cannot reach you, but you will run in, like Aaron with the censer of ministration,—there, where the poisoned darts fly thickest,—and at all risk, or even certainty, of suffering for yourself, will stand between the living and the dead. This is the spirit of the Lord Jesus ; the spirit of that faith which overcometh the world ; the spirit which, living and burning in the heart of Christ's faithful people in all ages, "determines to know nothing," in all its work and all its life, but "Jesus Christ and Him crucified."

SERMON XI.

Haggai, Zechariah, Malachi.

EZRA vi. 14.

"And the elders of the Jews builded, and they prospered through the prophesying of Haggai the prophet and Zechariah the son of Iddo. And they builded, and finished it, according to the commandment of the God of Israel, and according to the commandment of Cyrus, and Darius, and Artaxerxes king of Persia."

IN reading these words the question very naturally arises as to what part the prophets Haggai and Zechariah took in the secular and material work of building the Temple.

The previous verses record how Darius caused a search to be made in the house of the rolls at Babylon for the decree of Cyrus, which had been in abeyance for about twenty years through the opposition made to the rebuilding of the Temple by the adversaries of the Jews. The roll was discovered, and Darius at once confirmed and renewed all its provisions, commanding that without delay materials for the fabric, money for the payment of the workmen, and all that was required for the restoration of the service of the sanctuary, and the maintenance of the priests, should be supplied by the governors of the district at the king's cost, in order that they might offer sacrifices of sweet savour unto the God of heaven, and pray for the life of the king, and of his sons.

We are to note in this the fact that the imperial

power was responsible for the whole of the expense, and the imperial authority ordained by very severe penalties "the work to be done with all speed a." What more was wanted?

We read in the verse preceding the text that prompt obedience was paid to the decree. The governor on this side the river, and his companions, did speedily according to all that which Darius had sent. "And the elders of the Jews builded." They had the royal authority to encourage them, they were protected from their enemies, and money for the payment of the labourers was provided, and yet the inspired historian adds, "they prospered through the prophesying of Haggai the prophet and Zechariah the son of Iddo. And they builded, and finished it, according to the commandment of the God of Israel, and according to the commandment of Cyrus, and Darius, and Artaxerxes king of Persia." What is the inference we are to draw from this?

A great work was to be done for the national re-establishment of the worship of Almighty God. All that patronage, wealth, and power could do, was provided, but one thing was lacking, it was the spiritual element. The spiritual must co-operate with the secular, in order that success may attend the work. The governors and officers of the State might supply men, money, and materials, but until the religious feeling to obey the commandment of God, as well as the commandment of the king, was excited, the workmen would have had no heart in the building. The blessing of the Lord prospered their handiwork.

This reference to the influence excited by the prophets Haggai and Zechariah marks very plainly the

---

a Ezra vi. 12.

nature and object of the prophetic office. The word which God in time past spake by the mouth of His holy prophets was no empty sound or mystical foretelling of future events, the interpretation of which was to be found when the events were fulfilled; it was then what it is now, the voice of God to His Church stirring up zeal, and love, and faith, and obedience to every good word and work. It was the fresh spring of moral and religious life to the nation. And this is just what we shall find to have been the effect of the prophecies which have been selected for our consideration this evening.

For if we read and compare their writings with those of an earlier date, we shall not trace in these latter prophets of the old dispensation any evidence that the spirit of prophecy had degenerated from the time of Joel and Isaiah, or that the divine gift was gradually dying out; on the contrary, as the time drew near when a large portion of prophecy was to be accomplished, the predictions became, if possible, more plain, literal, and precise.

Take for example the last chapters of Malachi, which close with an unmistakeable prediction of St. John the Baptist, the messenger to prepare the way, and of Christ the Messenger of the covenant, to perfect the work of salvation.

In order, therefore, to mark the perfect harmony and identity and completeness of the divine inspiration, the four Evangelists commence their history with the event to which this prophecy refers. The last prophet of the Old Testament predicts the coming of the first prophet of the New. St. Mark, St. Luke, and St. John, in the first chapter, and St. Matthew in the third, refer to this. "The beginning of the Gospel of Jesus Christ the Son of

God; as it is written in the prophets, Behold I send My messenger before Thy face, which shall prepare Thy way before Thee." The indenture fits the original document, and proves that the Old Testament is not contrary to the New. Wherefore they are not to be heard which feign that the old Fathers did look only for transitory promises. The preaching of Haggai and of Zechariah in the time of Zerubbabel, and of Malachi in the time of Nehemiah, was as much the voice of God to the Church then as the preaching of John the Baptist was at the coming of Christ, or of the Apostles after the day of Pentecost. And this will be more plain, if we refer to a few details of the prophecies, in the order in which they are placed in Holy Scripture.

And, first, we find Haggai, in the second year of Darius, on the first day of the sixth month, reproving the indolence and selfishness of the people who said, "The time is not come that the Lord's house should be built," and who were furnishing and inhabiting their ceiled houses while the house of God laid waste. The appeal was not made in vain; we read in ver. 12, chap i., "Then Zerubbabel the son of Shealtiel, and Joshua the son of Jozedech the high-priest, with all the remnant of the people, obeyed the voice of the Lord their God, and the words of Haggai the prophet, as the Lord their God had sent him, and the people did fear before the Lord." In three and twenty days after the preaching of that sermon they commenced the work; there was a blessing upon it; the divine power was conveyed by the appeal to the congregation of Israel; there was an influence from above which did not exist before. We read, "The Lord stirred up the spirit of Zerubbabel, and the spirit of Joshua, and the spirit of all the remnant of the people, and they came and did work in the house of the Lord of Hosts their God." Feeble, then, was the commencement; the decree came from Darius, the will and the zeal to execute it from the God of heaven.

A month passed away, the work prospered, but the spirit of the people began to flag. As the building rose from the old ruins, they who saw the house in her first glory were moved to tears. It was in their eyes in comparison of it as nothing, and in their grief their hearts began to fail, their hands grew feeble, the work had well-nigh ceased. The Prophet is sent to encourage them. He tells them that although the outward appearance of their building might not equal that of former days, yet it should not be inferior in the divine favour, for the Lord had purposed to fill it with glory. "For the silver and the gold is mine," saith the Lord of Hosts. "The glory of this latter house shall be greater than of the former," saith the Lord of Hosts. Again, the divine Word raises their minds from the visible to the invisible, from the natural to the supernatural, "And the builders prospered through the prophesying of the prophet Haggai."

And next in chronological order we find the prophet Zechariah commencing his prophecy one month later than his predecessor. He had witnessed the laying of the foundations, and the zeal of the people, but as the work approached completion, his mission was to prepare the worshippers for the Temple, or rather to promote the building of the spiritual temple, to bring about a moral reformation, a religious revival among the people. In seven visions made to him on the night of the twenty-fourth day of the eleventh month the typical character and spiritual meaning of the Divine purpose towards the restored nation was revealed to him. Thus in good words, and comfortable words, he expounds the parable of the overthrow of the empires; the establishment of the worship of the true God; the sacredness of the office of the two anointed ones—the prince and the priest, who conjointly prefigured the Branch which should grow out of his place, who should build the Temple of the Lord, who should bear the glory, and should sit upon His throne, and be a priest upon his throne. With such heaven-sent teaching Zechariah put a real and spiritual significance upon the daily labour of the builders, and taught them that they were not labouring for time, but for eternity, and that their labour would not be in vain.

At the end of two years, when it seems the ordinances and discipline of the Temple worship had been resumed, certain Jews came to enquire whether the fasts of the fifth month in remembrance of the capture and desolation of Jerusalem by Nebuchadnezzar, which had been observed during the captivity, should be still observed. Zechariah is commissioned to tell the people that their mourning was turned into joy. The fasts of their exile were to be exchanged for cheerful feasts of joy and gladness. That what the Lord required was holiness of life. "Speak ye every man truth with his neighbour." "Execute the judgment of truth and peace in your gates." "Thus saith the Lord, I am returned unto Zion, and will dwell in the midst of Jerusalem; and Jerusalem shall be called a city of truth, and the mountain of the Lord of Hosts, the holy mountain." Zechariah nowhere encourages the pride of the nation with promises of worldly greatness: his object is to produce faith and holiness. When, therefore, he predicts the final glory of the kingdom, he preaches first the advent of Christ in humiliation; and, with a distinctness which no Jewish controversialist has ever been able to gainsay, describes the King who is God's fellow coming to the daughter of Jerusalem, "just and having salvation, lowly and riding upon an ass, and upon a colt the foal of an ass." Then he describes the value put upon Him by the nation; "the goodly price that He was prized at," and the potter's field which was purchased with the thirty pieces of silver. Then in wonderful words the manner of His death is set forth: "They shall look upon Me whom they have pierced." How the sword is awakened, how the Shepherd is smitten, the blood is shed, but "a bone of Him is not broken." Thus the "fountain was opened for sin and uncleanness," and the spirit of grace and supplications promised, trials and judgments shall prepare for the great and terrible day, when His feet shall again stand upon the Mount of Olives, and the Lord shall be King over all the earth.

With such evangelical teaching did the prophet prepare the people for the dedication of the Temple, and the reformation which for a few years was brought about by Ezra and Nehemiah. By his visions, by precept, and by prophecies, the Gospel of the grace of God was preached to the builders, "and they prospered through the prophesying of Zechariah the son of Iddo."

But, further—my text speaks of Artaxerxes, King of Persia, who began to reign about fifty years after the Temple was finished. What, then, is his connexion with the prophets Haggai and Zechariah? The book of Nehemiah supplies us with information which shews what must have been the moral state of the Jews during that period. For it seems that after the building and ordinances of the sanctuary had been restored, the religious excitement which had been awakened lasted but a short time, the people relapsed into a state of apathy. It is probable that the successor to Darius did not take the same interest in the welfare of the Jews, nor value the prayers of the Temple worshippers as his father had before him, and the voice of the prophets may have been silent; whatever may have been the cause, there is evident proof of religious declension. Mixed marriages with the border-nations, neglect of the Sabbath, oppression of the poor, and corruption both of doctrine and practice, and the seeds of those doctrines which were shortly to be developed in the rival sects of the Pharisees and Sadducees, were among the evils which marked the period when the Lord stirred up the spirit of Nehemiah to visit the city, and undertake the work of re-building its walls.

Nehemiah commenced his work in the second year of the reign of Artaxerxes, and having completed it, returned to Persia; then twelve years afterwards he returned to Jerusalem to reform the vices which had been fostered by a corrupt priesthood, and practised by a corrupted people. Notwithstanding all his zeal, authority, and pious example,—notwithstanding his courage, and self-denial, and unbending firmness in the cause of truth,—the civil governor failed to influence the people. He needed the higher influence of the prophets—the Ezra, the Zechariah, and the Malachi— to convince the disobedient of their error, and to encourage the good in holiness. As this was specially the mission of Malachi, he was the preacher to a backsliding people. It is highly probable that Malachi began to prophesy about the thirty-second year of Artaxerxes, when the Jews had been as long in possession of their religious ordinances, as they had been deprived of them during the captivity: seventy years of bondage had humbled them, seventy years of prosperity had puffed them up.

It must have been a melancholy and humiliating spectacle to the good Nehemiah, when he returned to Jerusalem the second time, to find Tobijah the Ammonite occupying an apartment in the holy Temple, the Levites deserting the house of God for the cultivation of their fields, and the tithe of oil and corn and wine not brought into the treasuries. It needed a sterner and more authoritative voice than that of the civil governor to awaken an unfaithful priesthood. The gentle and encouraging appeals of Zechariah were not suited to this state of things, the prophet's harp must strike a harsher chord; and thus we find Malachi by the word of the Lord rebuking the sins of the nation, as Elijah had done before, and as John the Baptist did after him. What civil governor would have ventured to utter such a denunciation as this to the ordained priests of the Temple: "And now, O ye priests, this commandment is for you. If ye will not hear, and if ye will not lay it to heart, to give glory to My Name, I will even send a curse upon you, and I will curse your blessings: yea, I have cursed them already, because ye do not lay it to heart. Behold, I will corrupt your seed, and spread dung upon your faces, even the dung of your solemn feasts; and one shall take you away with it." Who but an inspired prophet could have warned the Levites that because they had offered polluted bread upon the altar, and the sick and blind and lame for sacrifice, the Lord would make His Name great among the Gentiles? Who but one commissioned from above would answer the self-excusing question, "Will a man rob God?" with such a sweeping reply as this, "Ye have robbed me in tithes and offerings. Ye are cursed with a curse: even this whole nation." Who but one speaking in the power of the Holy Ghost could expose the unbelief and hypocrisy of the nation which professed to delight in the messenger of the covenant, and yet would not abide the day of His coming? Who in His first advent would be like "a refiner's fire and like fuller's soap," in His second advent as "a burning oven." Such was the closing testimony of the prophets to the Jewish nation. The last word of Malachi threatens with a curse, the first word of the Gospel is blessing.

And now what are the great lessons we are to learn from this review of the last canonical period of Jewish history.

1. The place which the spiritual element must occupy in all national and social organization for the good of the people. Laws may be passed to prohibit vice, schools may be instituted to educate the ignorant, a police force may be trained to detect and restrain offenders, and reformatories may be encouraged to reclaim criminals,—nay, there may be the outward framework of a Church, with its ministers and ordinances,— but if the voice of prophecy be silent, and the presence of God ignored, Phariseeism will take the place of religious power, and Sadduceeism sap the foundations of revealed truth. This was the teaching of Haggai: "Be strong all ye people of the land, for I am with you, saith the Lord of Hosts; My Spirit remaineth among you, fear ye not." And this was the teaching of Zechariah: "Not by might, nor by power, but by My Spirit, saith the Lord of Hosts." Secular power, Act of Parliament power, intellectual power, public opinion power, philanthropic power, have been tested and tried

to the uttermost, but no one of them, nor all of them put together, have ever succeeded in regenerating a nation or converting a soul. That people is on the high road to apostacy which teaches for doctrines the commandments of men.

2. But we learn, secondly, that the religious teaching must be of the right stamp. It must be revealed truth. Haggai, Zechariah, and Malachi preached by inspiration of God. They spake of Christ, they preached Christ; not a Socinian Christ, not an ideal Christ, not a spiritual Christ, but a personal, divine, and human and everliving Christ; One who is God's fellow, and yet meek and lowly, and more humble than the humblest of the sons of men; a Priest to offer sacrifice, and yet a King to rule all nations; a foundation-stone laid in tears, and yet "a top-stone put on with shoutings, crying, Grace, grace, unto it:" a pierced and bleeding sufferer, a living and glorious Judge of the whole earth. In these and similar statements, the great doctrines of the Incarnation, of the Atonement, of substitution, of imputed righteousness, of perfected salvation, are expressed; and by such motives it pleased God to mark the distinction between those who feared and served Him, and those who served Him not. The teaching of Scribes may expose and condemn all disobedience to the letter of the Divine Law, but conviction of sin will only be produced by the Gospel. "They shall look upon Me whom they have pierced, and mourn," is the language of the prophet of the Old Testament; "He shall convince of sin, because they believe not on Me," is the language of the New Testament. In both it is the work of the Holy Spirit. And is not this a matter of most deep and solemn importance in a day when the inspiration of prophets and the recorded facts of revelation are questioned and con-

tradicted? If we are to repent, and become as little children, that we may enter the kingdom of heaven, then is there but one way by which we may attain to this grace of humility. It is by the cross of Jesus we must win the crown: "Except a man be born of water, and of the Spirit, he cannot see the kingdom of God."

3. But, finally, when the outward organization has been established, the temple worship restored, the city walls re-built, civil and religious liberty secured, what shall be done if declension and backsliding come in upon a people? This is what took place in Jerusalem, this is what may occur again. St. Paul has spoken of a similar apostacy in the latter times, when "men shall be lovers of their own selves, covetous boasters, proud blasphemers, despisers of those that are good, heady, high-minded, lovers of pleasures more than lovers of God, having a form of godliness, but denying the power thereof." Where is the voice, loud, and bold, and strong enough to silence the adversaries, and convince the gainsayers? This is no imaginary hypothesis. There may be outwardly a blameless observance of the ceremonial, and yet inwardly a spirit of blasphemy, persecution, and injury. Where is the remedy to be found? What appeal can be made to awaken fear and arouse the torpid conscience? "Behold, the day cometh which shall burn like an oven" is no myth. The doctrine of everlasting punishment from the presence of the Lord is as certain as the hope of being with Him and like Him for ever. If Malachi's prophecy of the first advent found its literal fulfilment in John Baptist and the Lord Jesus, why should his awful prophecy of the second advent be ignored? "All the proud, yea, and all that do wickedly, shall be stubble, and the day that cometh shall burn them up, saith the Lord of Hosts; that it

shall leave them neither root nor branch. But unto you that fear My Name shall the Sun of righteousness arise with healing in His wings." This, then, is the great subject for the latter days of the Gentile as it was for the latter days of the Jewish dispensation. "The day of the Lord will come as a thief in the night." "The trumpet shall sound, and the dead shall be raised incorruptible." The final separation will be made between the sheep and the goats, the restitution of all things, the solution of all mysteries, the triumphs over sin, and death, and hell, and the establishment of a kingdom of righteousness and peace,—all this will be accomplished, and Jesus will be obeyed, and loved, and honoured—worshipped, adored, and praised—from sea to sea, and from pole to pole.

This is the last appeal. If this fails, all will fail. The rejection of the judgment to come is the wilful rejection of scoffers, walking after their own lusts, denying the Lord that bought them, and doing despite unto the Spirit of grace. For such, nothing remains but the blackness of darkness for ever. "Knowing the terrors of the Lord, we persuade men; for we must all appear before the judgment-seat of Christ, that every one may receive the things done in his body according to that he hath done, whether it be good or bad."

Such, my brethren, was the relation in which the spiritual element stood to the secular in the old dispensation, and such is its high and sacred position now. The powers that be are ordained of God. And although in the last days the democratic movement may supersede the monarchical system, and rationalism trample revelation under foot; although the two anointed witnesses, the Zerubbabel and the Joshua, the Church and the State, may witness in sackcloth;

yet they are witnesses for God, and the period of their trial is limited. The three and a-half days will speedily be accomplished, and their resurrection will usher in the last woe, when the seventh angel will proclaim the kingdoms of this world to be the kingdoms of our Lord and of His Christ, who will reign for ever and ever.

SERMON XII.

Enoch.

HEB. xi. 5.

"By faith Enoch was translated that he should not see death; and was not found, because God had translated him."

THESE words occur in the glowing description given by the Apostle of the triumphs of faith. After having defined this wonderful principle, he goes on to furnish these Hebrew Christians with certain familiar instances of its results and rewards. The first on the noble catalogue is that of Abel, whose accepted sacrifice (while that of Cain was rejected) proved his faith in the Divinely appointed method of salvation, and was a conspicuous type, in that early period, of the "Lamb of God that taketh away the sin of the world." The next example is that of ENOCH, of whom we are told in the text that "by faith he was translated, that he should not see death." He was translated by faith, because faith enabled him to please God, while his pleasing of God was the cause of his translation [a]. The Old Testament notices respecting Enoch are summed up in a few short verses in the fifth chapter of Genesis, a chapter which contains little more than a record of the generations of Adam. And yet, barren of interest though this chapter might at first seem, it is recorded somewhere of some penitent, that it was

[a] Πῶς δὲ πίστει μετετέθη; ὅτι τῆς μεταθέσεως ἡ εὐαρέστησις αἰτία, τῆς δὲ εὐαρεστήσεως ἡ πίστις.—St. Chrysostom.

the means of his conversion to God. That which affected him on reading this summary of human life was this, that the notice of each individual concludes with the words, "and he died." However long the life, it had an end; and this truth, through the power of God's grace, so wrought within him, that he resolved thenceforth so to live that he might not fear to die.

But is this chapter after all so very uninteresting? I read the record of these generations, and I ask myself how it was that the lives of these patriarchs were so marvellously prolonged. Some have supposed that this length of days was granted to them in order that the world might be sooner peopled, or that the knowledge of God might be better preserved. Others have thought that this protracted existence was a special mark of the Divine goodness vouchsafed to them on account of their piety. But though it is true that length of days is not unfrequently promised in Holy Scripture as the reward of piety, I nowhere read that a long life is a certain criterion by which to judge of the favour of God. Indeed the example of Enoch seems to point the other way; for he was removed from earth after a life comparatively short, and that, too, as a special reward for his holiness.

The real truth would seem to be this, that in the long lives of Adam and his immediate descendants, we may see the great and blessed gift of immortality, yet delaying, as it were, and retiring with reluctant footsteps, as though unwilling to withdraw itself from the creature for whom it had been designed. The gradual decline of man's life is an evidence of the original intention of God. Man in his condition of uprightness was destined for eternal life[b]. But no

[b] See Kalisch on Gen. v.

sooner had "sin entered the world, and death by sin," than those amazing physical powers which must have belonged to Adam in his state of innocence began gradually to deteriorate; and so, as one succession of the race after another was produced, it was propagated with something less of the original vigour. As generation succeeded generation, the vital force was gradually weakened; the contest with death became less and less equal; and so life shortened, and the days of man became fewer and fewer, until they had dwindled down from many centuries to threescore years and ten. It is well worthy of our notice to trace the gradual contraction of human life in the generations from Adam to Moses. The now forfeited immortality seems, as it slowly departed, to have flung its lingering shadow over those primæval men, as though to teach them from how high an estate they had fallen. And thus, when we read in this chapter the record of what appear to us such marvellous ages, we are forcibly reminded of that immortal state which was lost by sin, but which shall be recovered in the regeneration, when those who have been born anew in Christ, and have made their calling and election sure, shall cast off all marks of feebleness and imperfection; and "this mortal shall put on immortality," with powers and faculties even nobler than those which Adam lost; through Him who is "the Resurrection and the Life."

It is of course difficult for us, whose days are but "as it were a span long," to estimate fully the circumstances of those who lived in this early period, when man's days ran out to several hundreds of years. Enoch, the son of Jared, was the seventh in lineal descent from Adam; and yet Adam was not only alive when Enoch was born, but lived on till within sixty years of Enoch's translation. Again, Seth the son of Adam, born to him after his fall, was also living, and outlived the time of Enoch's removal many years. These facts alone are very interesting and suggestive. We picture to ourselves these grand old patriarchs, the mighty forefathers of our race, still handing on as living witnesses the traditions of our history from its beginning. There is Enoch with his six progenitors in direct succession, all living as his contemporaries, and in the fulness of their strength; and stretching back in an unbroken line, through what seems to us a dim vista of six hundred years, to the creation of Adam. Six centuries had passed since Adam was formed; and there Adam still was, with three hundred more years to run, when Enoch was born. Four hundred and fifty years had passed since the birth of Seth; and Seth had not then lived out half his days. What a wonderful fellowship must those early patriarchs have formed; of how much would they have to tell. We think of Adam's vast experience in his threefold condition of innocence, and transgression, and repentance unto life[e]. We think of Seth, the beginning of the holy seed from which the Second Adam was to spring, and of his son Enos, whose birth marked a new era, when men began to call on the name of Jehovah. And we may believe that as they "spake often one to another," those God-fearing men, and saw the gradual advances of Sin and Death in this fair creation, they were comforted with ever-brightening assurances of a coming day when all things shall be made new.

In such a companionship was the life of Enoch spent. But he lived in a far higher fellowship than this. His name is handed down to us with the brief but emphatic

[e] See Evans' "Scripture Biography."

eulogy that he "walked with God." Six hundred years of sin and evil had now done their work in the world; the stream of corruption was running broad and deep; and the time was approaching when God was about to send a flood of waters on the earth. In the midst of these aboundings of evil, and high above other examples of holiness, there towered up the noble character of Enoch, or the "Dedicated," as the word in the original implies. Less could not be affirmed of him, and hardly more could be added, to mark his saintly character, than this, that "Enoch walked with God." "Can two walk together," asks the Prophet, "except they be agreed [d]?" And this question carries with it its own self-evident reply. We know that in human relations there can be no hearty fellowship where there is no similarity of taste or feeling. There must be some congeniality in order to real friendship. And thus, comparing human things with Divine, we gather from this expression that the mind and heart of Enoch had been brought into agreement with his Creator; and this, again, implies that he had been wonderfully purified from sin, and endowed with affections which found their full satisfaction in God. He had become heavenly-minded. He loved what God delighted in, and hated what God abhorred. And as, day by day, he moved onwards in this blissful companionship, his heart was more and more lifted above the world, and fixed upon the "inheritance undefiled, and that fadeth not away." Nor was it only in moments of high aspiration and of deeper yearnings, such as I doubt not most of you have sometimes experienced, that he thus walked. It was the habit of his life, even in its most private and ordinary details. "Enoch lived," we read,

[d] Amos iii. 3.

"sixty-five years, and begat Methuselah. And Enoch walked with God after he begat Methuselah three hundred years." Did he walk with God the first sixty-five years of his life? Were his boyhood and his early manhood "dedicated" to God? We can hardly suppose it otherwise. But we may almost infer from the narrative, that if he walked with God before, the walking with his Creator became yet closer and more marked from that time. Yes; as his great and yet living progenitors communed with him, and as his family multiplied, still did he move in the world as the great pattern of undeviating, ever-increasing holiness. There was no slip, no painful discordance between his profession and his practice. Through no inconsiderable portion of the first great epoch of the world, from the Fall of Man to the Deluge, while "the wickedness of man was becoming great in the earth," there was at least one bright example to shew that even then the Holy Spirit strove with men; and that the human will was yet free to "refuse the evil and to choose the good." See, then, what faith wrought in Enoch, even its blessed fruits of a righteousness extending over at least three hundred years. Ah, brethren, when we compare our advantages with his, living as we do in the full light of the Gospel, and under all the influences of the ministration of the Spirit, and then contrast our fitful chequered life, our periods of better thought and holier endeavour, broken, alas! and interrupted by so many negligences and inconsistencies, with Enoch's stately and consistent march in holiness, are we not humbled by the reflection upon how much it wrought in him, compared with the little that it has produced in ourselves.

But Enoch was not merely a man of meditation; he was also a man of action. Our great philosopher, Lord

Bacon, says, speaking in reference to his example, that "for contemplation, which should be finished in itself, without casting its beams upon society, assuredly divinity knoweth it not[e]." And so Enoch was not contented only to exhibit a silent example of holiness; nor was his a life of mere dreamy abstraction. He opposed himself with great force and energy to the wickedness of that turbulent and atheistic age, and prophesied with no faltering accents of judgment to come. St. Jude tells us, speaking in reference to the profligates and unbelievers of his time, that "Enoch also, the seventh from Adam, prophesied of these, saying, Behold the Lord cometh with ten thousands of his saints; to execute judgment upon all; and to convince all that are ungodly among them of all their ungodly deeds which they have ungodly committed, and of all their hard *speeches* which ungodly sinners have spoken against him[f]."

You observe that in this quotation St. Jude speaks of Enoch as the "seventh from Adam." This may have been merely to mark the great antiquity of the prophecy, and to shew that in no age of the world has God left Himself without an outward and sensible witness to the second Advent of Christ. But may we not find in this expression a higher and deeper meaning? Seven is the number of completion and of rest. And in Enoch, thus taken in the seventh age from the strife and tumult of a wicked world to a holy rest, we seem to behold a type of that heavenly Sabbath which remains for the people of God[g]. Then, further, there was an Enoch in the race of Cain, the firstborn of the ungodly seed; and Cain built a city, and

[e] Bacon's "Advancement of Learning," book ii. [f] St. Jude 14, 15.
[g] See Wordsworth, *in loc*.

called it Enoch, or "the dedicated," after the name of his son. Thus the unholy build themselves up on the uncertain foundations of the life that now is. This is their "dedication," the beginning and the end of their life. But to the elect, Enoch is born, so to speak, in the seventh generation, because they look to the eternal city, the city which hath foundations, as their great and festal dedication. Therefore they now willingly bear poverty and reproach, and suffer worldly ills, that in the seventh age, that is, in the final retribution, they may be gloriously crowned [h].

But observe, further, the language of the prophecy, "Behold the LORD, i.e. JEHOVAH, cometh." Long, then, before the time of Moses was that mysterious name of Jehovah known. Enoch did not proclaim His coming merely as that of Elohim, the God of Providence, but as that of Jehovah, the covenant God, who in the fulness of time was to assume man's nature in Christ. And observe yet once more the words, "Behold, the Lord cometh!" They might be rendered according to the historic sense of prophecy, "Behold, the Lord *came!*" The Prophet sees the event as though it had already taken place. Full of the Spirit of God he predicted the coming of the Deluge then at hand, and not improbably prefigured in the name of his son Methuselah [i]. But he looked onwards also to that greater judgment

---

[h] "Hinc est, quod Cain primum filium Enoch vocat, atque ex ejus nomine civitatem, quam condidit, appellat. Enoch, quippe, *dedicatio* dicitur. Iniqui ergo se in primordiis dedicant; quia in hac vita quod ante est, cordis radicem plantant, ut hic ad votum floreant, et â sequenti patria arescant. Unde et e contra in electorum parte Enoch septimus oritur, quia eorum vitæ festa dedicatio in fine servatur," &c.—(*S. Gregorii,* in Genesim, vol. iv. p. 19.

[i] The word Methuselah in the original means, "man of offspring, or of sending forth (of waters)." He died, most probably, in the year that the Flood came.

of fire, of which this judgment of waters was a rehearsal. Gifted as he was with the spirit of prophecy, the intervening ages were in his estimate lessened to a point. His faith took firm hold on Christ, and overleaping what seems to us a vast interval of time, he saw and proclaimed the final overthrow of evil, and the glorious Advent of the Redeemer, sitting upon His throne, and girt about with the countless multitude of his saints.

But whence did St. Jude obtain this prophecy? There is indeed an Apocryphal book called the "Book of Enoch," with which many of the early Fathers were familiar. It was known to Justin Martyr, Irenæus, St. Augustine, and others, and was actually quoted by Tertullian. For several centuries this book disappeared from sight. But at the close of the last century, the well-known Oriental traveller, James Bruce, brought three copies of an entire Æthiopic translation of it from Abyssinia. This Æthiopic version, which was translated into English a few years ago by Archbishop Laurence[k], is apparently made from the Greek, the Greek itself being but a translation from a Hebrew original. For words and phrases occur in it of an evident Aramaic origin; and a Hebrew "Book of Enoch" was known and used by the Jews as late as the thirteenth century. The book would appear from internal evidence to have been written not earlier than the times of the Maccabees, or of Herod the Great, and not later than the early part of the second century. It was probably compiled from traditionary fragments, amongst which are to be found the words here quoted by St. Jude. We may on the whole infer that the pro-

[k] "The Book of Enoch," by Archbishop Laurence. (Oxford: J. H. Parker. 1838.)

phecy here imported into the Canonical Scriptures was a known and common tradition of the Jews, which St. Jude was Divinely guided to enshrine in the written Word of God ; and if so, there is something very striking in a floating tradition of twenty-five centuries being thus at last arrested, and fixed in the Canon, and so handed on as one of the inspired utterances of the great Prophet of old [1]. It shews how in every age the Second Advent is the one great event to which faithful men have looked, and around which their highest hopes and interests have revolved.

The life of Enoch was marked, then, by a constant walking with God, and by an active ministry against sin, in the preaching to that wicked age of the great truth of judgment to come. Faith enabled him to be true to God, and to overcome the world, whether in its frowns or in its smiles. Nor did it pass unrewarded. "He was not, for God took him." While yet "of middle

---

[1] Archbishop Laurence ("Book of Enoch," Oxford, 1838) is of opinion that this book was compiled in the time of Herod the Great. Professor Volkmar, of Zurich, contends, however, that it was written as late as A.D. 132, and thence raises a doubt as to the genuineness of the Epistle of St. Jude. This might be important, if it was necessary to suppose that the writer of that Epistle actually quoted from the "Book of Enoch." But the genuineness of St. Jude's Epistle is altogether unaffected by the date of this Apocryphal production, if with Dr. Lightfoot ("Harmony of the New Testament," p. 339,) we assume that St. Jude was "citing and referring to a known and common tradition" of the Jews.

One of the copies of the "Book of Enoch" brought home by Bruce was found by him amongst the books of Holy Scripture, standing immediately before the Book of Job, which, he adds, "is its proper place in the Abyssinian Canon." But all the early Fathers, excepting perhaps Tertullian, regard it as Apocryphal ; and even Tertullian admits that it was never received into the Jewish Canon : "Scio scripturam Enoch, non recipi a quibusdam, quia nec in armarium Judaicum admittitur."—(De cultu feminarum.)

For further information see Canon Westcott's Article in Dr. Smith's "Bible Dictionary," and Dean Alford's "Prolegomena on St. Jude."

age," for his life was short compared with those of his contemporaries, he vanished suddenly from earth. It may have been that in some moment, when with more than his wonted earnestness he was proclaiming the "odious truth" that Jehovah was coming to judge the world,—at some great crisis of evil, when he—

>―――― "spake much of right and wrong,
> Of justice, of religion, truth, and peace,
> And judgment from above, him old and young
> Exploded, and had seized with violent hands,
> Had not a cloud descending snatched him thence,
> Unseen amidst the throng ―――――――
> ――――――――――― to walk with God,
> High in salvation and the climes of bliss,
> Exempt from death, to shew (men) what reward
> Awaits the good; the rest what punishment [m]."

Silently, mysteriously, majestically, he passed away. Already "in heart and mind" he had ascended. He had moved on earth with so buoyant and elastic a step, with affections so fixed on heaven, that he was ready, when God was pleased to set him free, to soar upwards, like a liberated bird, to his heavenly home. And God took him away in body and soul, so that he passed from mortality to immortality without tasting death. Thus he shewed how it is possible for the body to live for ever and not see death. Thus also he became the type under the Patriarchal, as Elijah afterwards under the Jewish dispensation, of the Ascension of the glorified Body of Christ. Thus, moreover, he became the first-fruits of the saints who shall be found alive on the earth at the Second Advent. He was the first illustration of the truth more fully revealed in a later age; "we shall not all sleep, but we shall all be changed."

[m] Milton's "Paradise Lost," book xi. line 667, &c.

Such, my brethren, is the example of Enoch. And it teaches us this first, (1.) that that habit of life is most conducive to holiness which combines with active labours for God the opportunities of retirement and meditation. The contemplative life without action tends to make a man dreamy and unpractical. A busy, bustling life without reflection tends to make him worldly and secular. And here is one great temptation of these times. The world goes on so fast, and we live in such a whirl, that "things present" are too apt to absorb us. In an age so restless and feverish, albeit so full of life and action, we specially need to be reminded that true spirituality cannot well be maintained without appointed times for self-examination, for acts of penitence and of communing with our own hearts. And for this, our Sundays and other Holy Seasons, such as that through which we are now passing, are a great help. Happy are they who have been early taught and trained to spend these seasons well. They will find them to be "times of refreshing from the presence of the Lord." "They will go from strength to strength," till they reach the hill of Sion, and behold the fair beauty of the Lord.

Then (2.) secondly, the translation of Enoch reminds us that the body no less than the soul is redeemed by Christ. Shall we not then strive to glorify God in our bodies which are His? Shall not our bodies be watchfully maintained in their relation to the Body of Christ, the mind influencing the body, and the body obeying the sanctified will, till through the mercy of God they both are brought into a meetness for His presence Surely the cheerful open countenance, the calm contemplative brow, the mild expression of holiness, the genuine deep-seated smile of charity, are the evidences of a spiritual life, and the foreshadowings of the glorified body with which he who "walks with God" on earth shall hereafter be "clothed upon" in heaven.

But (3.) lastly, and above all, the ascending patriarch teaches us that we must first "walk with God" here, if we would walk with Him hereafter. Heaven is, indeed, but the consummation and perfection of that "walking with God" which commences on earth. If, then, you really hope for heaven, put this question honestly before you this night. Am I now in any measure walking with God? Am I desiring agreement with Him? Am I stedfastly resisting sin, overcoming infirmity, practising self-denial, loving what is true, and pure, and excellent? Am I submitting myself to the will of God, and using constantly the means which He has appointed for my sanctification, as prayer, and meditation, and Holy Communion? Am I "looking for that blessed hope, and the glorious appearing of the great God and our Saviour Jesus Christ?" If you can answer these questions hopefully, then may you trust that "He which hath begun a good work in you, will perform it until the day of Jesus Christ;" and having, like Enoch, walked with Him, it may be amidst trial and reproaches here, you shall be translated at the last to walk with Him amidst the glorious company of His saints, in bliss ineffable for evermore.

www.ingramcontent.com/pod-product-compliance
Lightning Source LLC
Chambersburg PA
CBHW020921230426
43666CB00008B/1527